S

Common Sense
APPROACH

Brenda O'Hanlon

Newleaf

Newleaf
an imprint of
Gill & Macmillan Ltd
Goldenbridge
Dublin 8
with associated companies throughout the world
© Brenda O'Hanlon 1998
0 7171 2628 5
Index compiled by Helen Litton
Design by Identikit Design Consultants, Dublin
Print origination by Carole Lynch
Printed by The Guernsey Press

This book is typeset in Revivial565 9.5pt on 15pt.

A catalogue record for this book is available
from the British Library.

1 3 5 4 2

Contents

While the author has made every effort to ensure that the information contained in this book is accurate, it should not be regarded as an alternative to professional medical advice. Readers should consult their general practitioners or physicians if they are concerned about aspects of their own health, and before embarking on any course of treatment. Neither the author, nor the publishers, can accept responsibility for any health problem resulting from using, or discontinuing, any of the drugs described here, or the self-help methods described.

Foreword

I t has been aptly said that to be alive is to be under stress. No life save one that has ended is stress-free. Or, as Brenda O'Hanlon simply puts it, stress is an integral part of life. How we cope with stress — be it in our personal, domestic lives or in the wider public arena — determines to a very significant extent the quality of our physical and our psychological health. It is, therefore, not so much a question of how to rid our life of stress as how to harness it, exploit it, control it.

That human beings appear to need some level of stress is noteworthy by what happens to those who are deprived of it. Contemporary research clearly indicates that people who lack stimulation and challenge, who are not exposed to the challenges that surge the adrenaline and race the pulse, soon seek them out. We are familiar with the notion of excess demand on our resources, causing stress such as work overload, emotional demands, social burdens. A lesser known, but equally valid, fact is that people who are *under-stimulated*, whose resources are not tested, who are not required to experience that sense of being stretched, also suffer the psychological symptoms of stress and manifest the behavioural and physiological characteristics that commonly accompany them.

To be stress-free, it would appear, means being in a state where our resources and the demands made on them are in perfect balance — but whenever we so much as approach such a state of stasis, we do something to disrupt the balance, to up the stakes.

Quite how an individual regulates the experience of stress in his or her life is itself affected by a host of factors, which include genetics; personality; early childhood experiences; the influence of parents, family, school, peers; social expectations; academic and occupational success. Ours is a society in which there is much complaining about stress and much living of the stressful life.

A young couple has no sooner taken out the mortgage their joint incomes can support when they move to a bigger, more expensive house or start a family, or both. The mountain climber who climbs Mont Blanc with a guide, then decides to do it alone. The business manager coping well with a department under her control opts to take on the challenge of an entire division. Human kind cannot seem to bear the stress-free state, and no person or group is particularly happy being described as completely unstressed!

In my career as a psychiatrist, I am often asked to talk to this or that professional group, trade or occupation about stress and its management — teachers, students, bankers, managers, doctors, lawyers, editors, dentists, farmers, politicians, priests, nuns, publicans, engineers. No group would wish to be described as neurotic or psychiatrically disordered, but each loudly insists it is under immense stress and, indeed, believes that this is a new phenomenon. There is much nostalgic talk of an earlier, less stressful, more serene age.

Clearly there is status in stress — in the work area, particularly; if you are not stressed, this may be interpreted as meaning you are not doing enough. However, what we have learned from occupational stress is the extent to which it is related to control. Those occupations in which control over work demands is lacking — one thinks especially of secretaries and telephonists — are particularly marked by serious levels of stress.

Control is an important word when it comes to stress. Feeling out of control is one of the earliest signs of someone breaking under stress. Being in control protects against such a breakdown. Much stress is either overload or burnout; in either case, the individual feels that he or she is not in control of what is happening, is responding to rather than calling the shots. Much of stress management amounts to little more than restoring the individual's sense of being in control — of their physiological and psychological responses; of their immediate personal lives; of their wider social and public duties and responsibilities.

Crucial to this sense of control is the possession of knowledge, information, the facts. The commonest complaint of someone under stress is that they do not understand what is happening to them — the strange physical sensations and psychological fears and apprehensions; the deterioration in personal and social functioning; the sense of impending disintegration and even doom.

Individuals who are familiar with the physical sensations that accompany excess (or indeed insufficient) physical exertion, are bewildered by those that accompany excessive or insufficient psychological demands. Thus, many people are still astonished that stress can manifest itself in poor sleep, impaired concentration, deteriorating memory, palpitations, stomach churning, dizziness, numbness of hands and feet, throat tightening, difficulty breathing and so forth, and assume that there must be some physical cause — cancer, heart disease, asthma — to explain how they feel. The fact that so many medical conditions are provoked or aggravated by stress complicates the picture still further.

In this book, Brenda O'Hanlon, recognising that much stress can be managed by the individual concerned without recourse to professional experts, conventional therapists, alternative practitioners and the massed armies of counsellors, guides and healers which are a feature of our post-Freudian age, lays out in a way that is both accessible and reliable what is currently known about stress and can be implemented by an individual of average intelligence.

If a person does need to seek outside help — and there is guidance here as to how such a decision might be made — then sensible advice is provided as to how one might make sense of the therapeutic pot-pourri on offer. What is on offer is truly bewildering in its variety and effectiveness. The author's intention is to provide as exhaustive and useful an account of what is available for the reader who wishes to be in greater control of the stressful demands in life, and in that regard she has succeeded and succeeded admirably.

Professor Anthony Clare
Medical Director, St Patrick's Hospital, Dublin
Former Professor of Psychological Medicine,
    St Bartholomew's Hospital, London

Did You Know That ... ?

- An estimated forty million working days are lost each year in the UK as a result of stress.
- Research carried out in the US indicates that nine out of ten people report experiencing high levels of stress often, with six out of ten claiming to be under great stress at least once a week.
- Stress-related problems account for more than six out of ten visits to doctors' surgeries.
- A number of studies have shown that loss-related life events — such as the death of a husband, relative or friend — may be implicated in the development of breast cancer, particularly in women who have difficulty expressing their feelings.
- A stressful life style is believed to be one of the main reasons why women doctors die on average ten years younger than male doctors.
- Suicide statistics for professions such as dentists, vets and doctors show rates two to three times higher than the general population.
- Anxiety, depression, neuroses, addiction to alcohol and other drugs are all clearly associated with stress.
- The type of stress that produces feelings of worry, sadness and frustration is linked with increasing levels of glucose in the blood.
- Tension and hypertension (high blood pressure) are not the same thing. You can have high blood pressure without feeling tense. Continual stress may, however, lead to high blood pressure.

◆ If you ignore stress, you may develop a serious physical or medical condition, or a more debilitating emotional problem, thereby adversely affecting your quality of life.

◆ Stressed and contracted muscles in one area have a knock-on effect in other parts of the body. If not dealt with, something like a frequently clenched jaw can cause referred pain, leading to neck and back trouble.

◆ Exposure to long-term stress in a sensitised person stimulates, and may eventually alter, the physical patterns of the brain. Once sensitised, people do not respond to stress in the same way from then on. The most trivial events can produce extreme reactions.

◆ Research suggests that prolonged stress affects the immune system, possibly facilitating the development of cancer.

◆ Stress raises serum cholesterol and blood pressure, and renders the arteries more susceptible to spasms that may trigger heart attacks and strokes.

◆ Death from cardiovascular disease, including heart attacks and strokes, is the most common cause of premature death in developed countries.

◆ The relaxant Diazepam is the fourth most commonly prescribed drug.

CHAPTER 1

All About Stress

S tress is an integral part of life. Avoiding stress isn't always either possible or desirable — it can be very beneficial. Where it becomes a problem is whenever we lose control: whenever pressure increases, but the ability to deliver does not.

Stress is truly unique to every individual. One person's stress is literally another person's adrenaline. Some people thrive on it — racing drivers, pilots, members of certain branches of the police and armed forces, television broadcasters, actors, journalists as well as others in the arts, performance and communication fields, and those in business/management.

Negative stress occurs whenever we perceive a given situation as threatening, emotionally disturbing or disquieting, rather than challenging; whenever there's an imbalance between the demands that are placed on us and our perceived capacity to cope. If you have been subjected to prolonged stress without realising it, it may take only a relatively minor incident to tip the balance, setting off the chain reaction that leads to a full-blown dramatic stress response. Stress is a bit like a dripping tap — just one extra drop and the whole system overflows.

Flight, Fright or Fight

We are all conditioned as human beings to respond in one of three ways to stress. These are known as the flight, fright or fight responses, and they have at their root a physiological reaction triggered in the brain.

The body cannot tell the difference between everyday stressors like being late for an appointment, or burning a saucepan, and major stressors like being involved in a road accident, or being threatened by a burglar. It responds the same way, regardless, by unleashing a flood of hormones including adrenaline, noradrenaline and cortisol.

Muscles throughout the body then tense; blood rushes to the heart, so the heart rate goes up. At the same time, glucose is released to provide energy. Blood supply is diverted from the gut, so digestion slows down, or stops. Blood supply is also diverted from the skin and extremities, so hands and feet go cold, discoloured or sweaty, and start shaking. The mouth goes dry, as saliva flow stops. The air spaces in the lungs dilate, so breathing becomes faster. The pupils dilate, the hair stands on end. The anal and bladder muscles relax and contract — alternately creating the urge to urinate or causing diarrhoea.

The effects of adrenaline release aren't entirely negative, however. In moments of great danger, it helps survival by mobilising sugars to give the body more strength, energy and stamina, thereby enabling us to fight harder or run faster — bracing us for action. With reduced blood supply to the skin and the inessential organs, bleeding is minimised in cases of injury, and energy isn't wasted on processes not immediately useful. Nausea or diarrhoea may also occur as the body eliminates the excess weight that might otherwise slow it down.

In most people, once the moment of danger has passed, they recover. The body warms up, the dry mouth disappears and adrenaline drains from muscles throughout the body: equilibrium is restored.

Typical examples of one-off, harmless, stress-inducing situations include speaking in public, doing an exam or driving test. People subjected to frequent or *prolonged* stress, however, may lose the ability to process stress-induced physical symptoms. They remain poised for action, on red alert, in a state of semi-arousal. A body maintained at that level is like a highly tuned engine. It takes very little additional pressure to tip the balance. Over-reactions to even small stressors may occur. Road rage is a graphic example of over-reaction.

Pre-Disposition to Stress

Several factors determine your pre-disposition to stress. It depends on each individual's personality, coping skills, self-esteem, self-confidence, social support, physical stamina and overall general health. The stress-hardy personality, who has good coping skills and does physical exercise, will be more resistant than somebody who is driving themselves hard, drinking and smoking in order to cope, and who has stopped taking physical exercise.

Self-esteem is one of the most crucial elements in a person's anti-stress armoury. It influences attitude, which in turn affects reactions to stress. Unemployment, or a constant feeling of helplessness, can cause low self-esteem. That kind of chronic stress can upset endocrine balance, causing the release of cortisol, an immune system suppressing hormone, which in turn lowers resistance to infection and illness.

On the other hand, people who feel in control of their lives can withstand what might appear to others to be unbearable stress. Air traffic controllers are a case in point. A recent study carried out among the large workforce of a very busy airport found that air traffic controllers were among the least stressed, while airport cleaners reported a high level of stress. Not surprisingly, *their* attitude to their jobs — how they perceived themselves, coupled with factors such as the never-ending nature of their jobs — all combined to create a negative, pessimistic and unconfident outlook. Their psychological outlook was in turn reflected in a high rate of stress-related illnesses.

What this and many other scientific studies show, is that those who have negative, pessimistic, extreme or unconfident outlooks, and who feel they have no control over their lives, fare worst. They become what they think they are; what they expect to happen tends to happen. Those with maximum control have a completely different and more positive outlook. They also become what they think they are; what they expect will happen tends to happen. In overall health terms, they fare best.

Chronic Stress and Illness

If you are suffering from chronic long-term stress, the chances are that your outlook will be negative and pessimistic. So the obvious question, then, is: can illness be far behind? Long-term stress may be at the root of serious illness. It is implicated in accidents as well as a range of psycho-social problems. The list that follows spells all this out starkly. These health problems, some of which are serious, are all recognised to have stress associations:

- alcohol and drug abuse
- allergies
- anxiety
- asthma (certain kinds)
- back and other musculo-skeletal problems
- colitis
- constipation
- coronary thrombosis (heart attack)
- depression
- diabetes mellitus
- flatulence
- hay fever
- headaches
- hypertension (high blood pressure)
- hyperthyroidism/under-active thyroid gland
- indigestion
- inflammatory bowel diseases
- irritable bowel syndrome
- itching
- menstrual difficulties
- migraine
- nervous dyspepsia
- peptic ulcers
- pruritis
- rheumatoid arthritis
- skin disorders (including eczema, hives and acne)
- sleeping problems
- tuberculosis.

Apart from these specific problems, stress has other insidious links — some proven, others suspected — with illness. Many researchers believe there is a direct link between psycho-social events and the immune system. Stress depresses the immune system, which in turn leaves the body vulnerable to the kinds of diseases already described, as well as serious conditions such as recurrent infections. That link, and the suppression of certain antibodies, may also explain why we double our risk of catching a cold if we are under stress.

Cancer is increasingly being linked to life style factors. There is no conclusive evidence that stress is part of the cancer inducing equation. However, some experts believe there is a link.

The hormones adrenaline and noradrenaline, released into the bloodstream during stressful periods, lay down plaque. When under stress, the body also releases fats. These increase the level of cholesterol in the body, and may also cause arterial plaque, ultimately leading to hardening of the arteries. Both are among the many factors implicated in the cause of coronary heart disease.

Stress can disrupt the hormonal balance in women, and may interfere with the reproductive system. It can also affect menstruation and fertility.

Because stress interferes with blood distribution through-out the body, logically, therefore, prolonged stress must impact on growth, cell development and repair.

Stress affects the areas of the brain that also control eating, aggression and sleep. Stress hormones affect the release of sero-tonin, and are specifically implicated in major behavioural changes, such as depression and sleeping problems.

Exposure to stress causes the brain to increase the release of cortisol, which affects the metabolism of carbohydrates and protein. Shifts in cortisol production may in turn lead to obesity or affect the body's ability to fight inflammation. Excess cortisol can cause women to develop masculine traits. High levels of cortisol can also have a negative effect on concentration and attention, resulting in poor short-term memory, forgetfulness and poor decision-making. If someone is agitated and disturbed, his or her brain's ability to take in new information may be diminished. As a result, work production and overall performance may decrease.

Stress or Medical Illness?

According to Dr Abbie Lane, a consultant psychiatrist specialising in stress management at the Dublin County Stress Clinic, stress doesn't form a neat package. Often its diagnosis is based on ruling out other causes. A lot of stress symptoms could point towards serious medical illness.

Certain medical conditions, such as an overactive thyroid, may mimic stress symptoms (palpitations, sweatiness, cold hands and feet, jitteriness, irritability and difficulty sleeping). Nausea or flatulence may indicate peptic ulcers, while headaches could indicate a more serious brain problem. Some coronary heart disease symptoms (breathlessness, palpitations, dizziness, nausea and faintness) also mimic stress, so it's important, adds Dr Lane, that people consult a medical doctor to rule out the possibility of a physiological cause.

Sleep disturbance is most commonly stress- or anxiety-related, but it may also be caused by physiological, physical, pharmacological or environmental factors. (See *Sleep: The CommonSense Approach* for details of these factors.)

The Good News

The good news about stress is that it is very treatable. It is not a condition for life — it just requires basic changes in life style, nothing remarkable. It is, of course, better not to become a victim of severe stress in the first place. As already outlined, certain things protect against stress:

- confidantes (paid or otherwise)
- efficient time management
- exercise
- goal setting
- keeping things in perspective
- regular breaks
- regular life style — a good diet, low alcohol consumption and avoiding smoking
- relaxation
- supportive relationships.

There is a direct correlation between the amount of stress we're under and productivity. Approaching deadlines focus our attention, so productivity increases. But there is a level beyond which any additional stress is not productive. At that stage, *good* stress becomes *dis*tress and related behaviours begin to manifest. These include irrationality; irritability; inability to prioritise; sleep disturbance; lethargy; apathy; aggression; panic; anxiety; and, eventually, depression and burn-out.

CHAPTER 2

Life Event Crises — the Pecking Order

The concept of the impact different life crises may have on subsequent illness is an extremely interesting one. The theory is that a high score on the league table of specific life events in any previous two-year period indicates a high probability of mental or physical illness relatively shortly afterwards.

For example, a total score of 300 indicates an eighty per cent likelihood of illness arising. For a score of between 200 and 299, the likelihood is fifty per cent, and for scores of between 150 and 199, it is thirty-three per cent. None of this is cast in stone, however. Individual responses and situations will be as complex as they are varied. If a person has in place a sufficient number of the buffers and coping skills as described by Dr Lane, then the likelihood of illness reduces.

The table that follows indicates the pecking order of life crises as identified by doctors T. H. Holmes and R. H. Rahe, who have carried out pioneering work in this area. For the layperson, one of the surprising things is that events that might at first glance appear to be positive experiences can be stressors, to a greater or lesser extent. Marriage, marital reconciliation, an outstanding personal achievement, the birth of a child, Christmas and holidays all fall into that particular category. As Professor Cary Cooper, one of the world's leading experts on stress, says, whether the event is favourable or unfavourable, competitive or complementary, is immaterial.

The Life Crisis Scoring Table

Event	Points
Death of a husband or wife	100
Divorce	73
Marital separation	65
Jail term	63
Death of a close family member	63
Personal illness or injury	53
Marriage	50
Job loss	47
Marital reconciliation	45
Retirement	45
Serious illness	44
Pregnancy	40
Sexual difficulties	39
Birth, adoption of a new baby, or older person moving into the home	39
Merger, business re-organisation, or bankruptcy	38
Change in financial state (either a lot better or a lot worse off)	38
Death of close friend	37
More arguments with family or spouse	35
A large mortgage or loan	30
Legal action over a debt	30
Change in responsibilities at work — promotion/demotion/lateral move	29
Son or daughter leaving home	29
Trouble with in-laws	29
Outstanding personal achievement	28
Spouse begins or stops work	26
Beginning or end of school or college	26
Change in living conditions	25
Change in personal habits	24

Event	Points
Trouble with boss	23
Change in working hours or conditions	20
Moving house	20
Change in school or college	20
Change in recreation	19
Change in social activities	19
A small loan or mortgage	17
Change in sleeping habits (either sleeping a lot more or a lot less)	16
Change in eating habits (either eating a lot more or a lot less, or eating at erratic hours)	15
Change in amount of contact with family	15
Holiday	13
Christmas	12
Minor violations of the law	11

Since this scale was originally developed by Doctors Holmes and Rahe many years ago, Professor Cary Cooper and a team of researchers have developed a new system, which uses individuals' perceptions of various life events to determine their degree of upset or stress reaction. Although they have some similarities, the two tables are actually quite different. Some people prefer the original, because subjectivity is not part of the scoring measurement process.

The advantage of testing yourself on either the Holmes and Rahe Scale, or the Cooper, Cooper and Cheang Life Events Scale — and identifying what your big life event stressors are — is that this may help anticipate possible negative reactions to events. Knowing your total score, and understanding and recognising the relative significance of each individual life event may flag you on the need to prepare to put stress management techniques in place.

Alternatively, it may mean looking at making a number of life style adjustments, such as cutting back on working hours, or

Stress

postponing a house move. Or it might simply indicate the need to take more care of yourself generally in terms of diet, nutrition, exercise, rest, relaxation and recreation.

The questionnaire that follows is reproduced from *Living with Stress*, by Cary L. Cooper, Rachel D. Cooper and Lynn H. Eaker, reproduced by kind permission of Penguin UK. It uses the aforementioned individuals' perceptions measurement scale to assess the impact of those life events.

Life Events: Subjective Assessment

Place a cross, X, in the Yes column for each event which has taken place in the last two years. Then circle a number on the scale which best describes how upsetting the event crossed was to you; e.g. 10 for death of a spouse.

Event	Yes	Scale
Bought house		1 2 3 4 5 6 7 8 9 10
Sold house		1 2 3 4 5 6 7 8 9 10
Moved house		1 2 3 4 5 6 7 8 9 10
Major house renovation		1 2 3 4 5 6 7 8 9 10
Separation from loved one		1 2 3 4 5 6 7 8 9 10
End of relationship		1 2 3 4 5 6 7 8 9 10
Got engaged		1 2 3 4 5 6 7 8 9 10
Got married		1 2 3 4 5 6 7 8 9 10
Marital problem		1 2 3 4 5 6 7 8 9 10
Awaiting divorce		1 2 3 4 5 6 7 8 9 10
Divorce		1 2 3 4 5 6 7 8 9 10
Child started school/nursery		1 2 3 4 5 6 7 8 9 10
Increased nursing responsibilities for elderly or sick person		1 2 3 4 5 6 7 8 9 10
Problems with relatives		1 2 3 4 5 6 7 8 9 10
Problems with friends/neighbours		1 2 3 4 5 6 7 8 9 10
Pet-related problems		1 2 3 4 5 6 7 8 9 10
Work-related problems		1 2 3 4 5 6 7 8 9 10
Change in nature of work		1 2 3 4 5 6 7 8 9 10

Stress

Event	Yes	Scale
Threat of redundancy		1 2 3 4 5 6 7 8 9 10
Changed job		1 2 3 4 5 6 7 8 9 10
Made redundant		1 2 3 4 5 6 7 8 9 10
Unemployed		1 2 3 4 5 6 7 8 9 10
Retired		1 2 3 4 5 6 7 8 9 10
Increased or new bank loan/mortgage		1 2 3 4 5 6 7 8 9 10
Financial difficulty		1 2 3 4 5 6 7 8 9 10
Insurance problem		1 2 3 4 5 6 7 8 9 10
Legal problem		1 2 3 4 5 6 7 8 9 10
Emotional or physical illness of close family or relative		1 2 3 4 5 6 7 8 9 10
Serious illness of close family or relative requiring hospitalisation		1 2 3 4 5 6 7 8 9 10
Surgical operation experienced by family member or relative		1 2 3 4 5 6 7 8 9 10
Death of husband		1 2 3 4 5 6 7 8 9 10
Death of family member or relative		1 2 3 4 5 6 7 8 9 10
Death of close friend		1 2 3 4 5 6 7 8 9 10
Emotional or physical illness of yourself		1 2 3 4 5 6 7 8 9 10
Serious illness requiring your own hospitalisation		1 2 3 4 5 6 7 8 9 10
Surgical operation on yourself		1 2 3 4 5 6 7 8 9 10
Pregnancy		1 2 3 4 5 6 7 8 9 10
Birth of baby		1 2 3 4 5 6 7 8 9 10
Birth of grandchild		1 2 3 4 5 6 7 8 9 10
Family member left home		1 2 3 4 5 6 7 8 9 10
Difficult relationship with children		1 2 3 4 5 6 7 8 9 10
Difficult relationship with parents		1 2 3 4 5 6 7 8 9 10

Plot total score below

Low Stress   **High Stress**

1_____50_____100

CHAPTER 3

Behaviour/Personality Types and the Stress Equation

Some personality types fare worse than others in the war against stress, and its links to certain major illnesses. People with Type A behaviour fare worst of all. For example, among this group, the incidence of cardiac illness/death from premature heart attack is extremely high. Unfortunately, not enough people realise early enough that with the right kind of life style modifications, the onset of chronic illness could be avoided, or at least delayed. Cardiovascular disease is itself the single biggest cause of premature death in the West.

Type A Personality

Type A behaviour was first identified in the 1960s, by Dr Meyer Friedman, a San Francisco cardiologist. One day, his office cleaner remarked that the seats of the chairs his patients used were remarkably worn at the edges. The reason was simple: Dr Friedman's patients, by and large, tended to sit *literally* on the edge of their seats. They were, overall, very tense. The cleaner's observation sparked a thought process that led Dr Friedman to interview the widows of those of his patients who had sub-sequently died of heart attacks. From the information they gave him about their husbands' life styles and personality traits, coupled with other research and observations of his own, he isolated a number of key differentiating characteristics and behaviours believed to be linked to the onset of cardiac illness/heart attack.

Patients who could be described as aggressive, aggravated, impatient and irritable were the most at risk. Other common traits among certain coronary heart disease patients were that they tended to push themselves hard; achieved a lot/got a lot of things done, but were often difficult to live with.

To further confirm Friedman's belief that certain traits/behaviours were factors implicated in the cause of heart attack, he decided to conduct an experiment on his own patients. He gave one half conventional treatment; he put the second half through a course of philosophical engineering. He introduced this second group to poetry and humour; he gave them a different way of thinking and living, as well as guidelines on relating to people in a less stress-inducing way.

Many months later, Dr Friedman sat both groups down to a very fatty meal. Later, he tested their blood. Among other things, he found that the first group absorbed cholesterol in a quite different way from the second group. In the first group, the cholesterol remained in the blood for a long time afterwards. In the second group, the blood colour returned to its normal bright red within twenty minutes, because this group metabolised fat more quickly.

It wasn't that the first group had ingested *more* cholesterol. The critical factor was that their adrenaline system wouldn't permit them to break it down as well. Digestion works better if you are relaxed, which they were not.

Stress-Inducing Behaviour

The following are thumbnail sketches of typical Type A behaviour. Some of this is maladaptive, some of it positive. In general, Type As:

◆ are demanding of themselves and others
◆ are impatient and resentful when other people do things more slowly than they would like; tend to finish other people's sentences

- are inclined to bursts of aggression and anger that surprise even themselves
- bottle up resentment
- can be bossy
- constantly feel they should be achieving more than they already have achieved
- feel on edge a lot of the time
- feel they have to do everything themselves; are not good at delegating
- find life a very aggravating and frustrating experience; have no sense of peace
- push themselves, and push against the tide of events
- lacking tolerance and patience, they find it difficult to engage productively with people to resolve conflicts or problems.

On the plus side, successful business people, entrepreneurs and leaders of all kinds may display more Type A behaviour traits. This makes them more task-oriented than other people, so they tend to achieve a great deal, while perhaps stepping on a number of toes along the way.

Type B Behaviour

In contrast, people exhibiting with Type B behaviour:

- are able to let go of things
- are more accepting of themselves, of others and of reality
- are more forgiving of themselves for failure
- are not excessively demanding
- don't have a problem confronting people, if there are difficulties to be faced
- like working with people
- relate well to people
- take time to process what is going on, and if there are problems will look at the issues.

Any of us can manifest with either type of behaviour, depending on the situation. Typically stressed individuals display more Type A than Type B behaviour, but this is only regarded as abnormal if it becomes a continuous pattern.

Of the two, Type B is the healthier option. It should be emphasised, however, that people are rarely exclusively either A or B. A combination of the two is usual, with people switching from one behaviour to the other (even during the same day), depending on circumstances and the levels of stress they are experiencing.

Other personality types prone to maladaptive stress behaviours are the Anxious Type and the Perfectionist Type.

The Anxious Type

This type of personality has the following particular traits:

◆ imagines the worst is going to happen
◆ sees danger everywhere
◆ tends to be hyper-vigilant — always on the lookout for something in their immediate environment that might signal problems
◆ worries in anticipation of events.

The Perfectionist Type

◆ has excessive expectations of self and others
◆ is unaccepting and critical of own failures and the failures of others.

This book is designed to help people to devise strategies for bringing the negative aspects of Type A behaviour more into line with the healthier option, Type B.

CHAPTER 4

Are You In Trouble?

S tress overload may manifest in a number of symptoms:

◆ physical
◆ emotional/mental
◆ behavioural.

A simple way to see how you are faring is to keep a diary for two or three weeks. At quarter- or half-day intervals, log one-line descriptions of your predominant emotions, physical reactions and behaviours in those time frames.

The following example may be helpful.

Monday

	Activity	**Thoughts**	**Behaviour**
Morning	Typing report that should have been done a week ago. *or* Sick child, school run, washing machine breaks down.	Worrying about dead-lines and other tasks to be completed; wondering what to do next.	Impatient, irritable, rush-ing, making mistakes, anxious, panicky.
Lunch	Sandwich at desk. *or* Tea, bread and yoghurt stand-ing in kitchen.	Outstanding jobs; waiting for people to call.	Rushed, eating fast.

Monday

	Activity	Thoughts	Behaviour
Afternoon	Report finished; returned phone calls; sent off three reports. *or* Back from doctor; washing machine fixed; someone else doing school run.	Getting things done at last.	Organised, relieved.
Evening	Dinner and walk; feet up, reading newspaper for first time.	Feeling good; thinking about the weekend.	Happy, smiling, relaxed.

It is important to track all three strands — emotional, physical and behavioural — simultaneously. The pages that follow provide a checklist of what type of predominant symptoms to look out for. If several of these symptoms have been present for *some weeks*, you may need to consult your doctor, to eliminate the possibility of a physiological cause. He or she should be able to identify why you feel under par.

If stress *is* the underlying cause, then you really do need to put a stress management programme in place. If you ignore it, you could develop a serious physical or medical condition, or a more debilitating emotional problem.

Physical Symptoms of Stress

These are wide-ranging, and may often appear not to be interconnected. For example, it would not be unusual for someone to be investigated by a neurologist (for migraine); by a genitourinary specialist (for bladder problems); a cardiologist (for palpitations), or an allergy specialist (for asthma) without ever making the stress connection.

The classic physical symptoms list is as follows:

- appetite change
- asthma (a complicated illness, but one which is sometimes aggravated by stress)
- cold hands and feet, or cool skin
- chronic constipation
- chronic diarrhoea
- dizziness
- dry mouth
- excessive sweating
- facial muscle twitches or tics
- frequency (desire to urinate)
- frequent colds, flu or other infections
- high pitched or choking voice
- increased sensitivity/irritable reaction to noise
- indigestion
- intense and long-term tiredness
- irregular breathing and breathlessness, even without physical exertion
- migraine
- muscle tension or slight pains in the chest, stomach, shoulders, neck and jaws (the last sometimes manifesting as bruxism, night-time grinding of the teeth), clenched fists
- nausea
- obesity
- palpitations — throbbing heart
- restlessness and fidgeting
- sexual problems, such as impotence
- shakiness
- skin irritation or rashes
- sleeping difficulties (either in falling asleep, staying asleep, or early morning wakening)
- stomach ache/tummy butterflies
- susceptibility to allergies
- vague aches and pains as well as backache, neck ache, abdominal pain and headache
- weight gain or loss.

Emotional/Mental Symptoms of Stress

There's a world of difference between the survival stress reactions that occur before a job interview, giving a speech or some other short-term anxiety-provoking scenario, and the type of stress reaction caused by long-term exposure to difficult situations.

Unrecognised and unattended to, these reactions may gradually erode your quality of life, and wreck relationships with work colleagues, family and friends. As a result, people may find themselves isolated, with few social outlets. Because they feel stressed, they have little or no desire to socialise. They make excuses for not going out, so their phone stops ringing. The social isolation then gets worse, and so a vicious cycle evolves.

The range of emotional symptoms may include: feeling tense, nervous, apprehensive or anxious; displaying increased suspiciousness, gloominess, fussiness, lack of enthusiasm, or cynical/inappropriate humour; feeling alienated, dissatisfied with life, de-motivated, or less confident; manifesting with reduced self-esteem; feeling under attack; and expressing job dissatisfaction.

Reactions may manifest in a number of psychological/ mental problems. The most serious of these are anxiety, panic attacks and depression, with or without suicidal tendencies.

Less serious, but none the less upsetting, are the following:

◆ acting defensively, or aggressively
◆ being overly critical
◆ being disorganised
◆ being less intuitive and less sensitive
◆ difficulty making decisions
◆ difficulty remembering recent events
◆ difficulty working equipment, or carrying out simple tasks
◆ feeling frustrated with people

- having difficulty taking in new information
- inability to concentrate
- irrational or rash decision-making
- irritability or impatience — interrupting others
- lack of physical co-ordination or tendency to be accident prone
- making more mistakes
- relying more on medication
- sleeping problems, including lying awake worrying about the next day, or having bad dreams
- tunnel vision.

Behavioural Symptoms of Stress

These include:

- anti-social behaviour, such as arguing in public, or being insensitive to others
- claiming to be too busy to relax
- driving badly
- eating in a hurry
- experiencing increased problems at home
- inability to unwind
- loss of interest in sex
- low productivity
- managing time badly
- not looking after yourself
- restlessness
- smoking or drinking more
- taking work home more, or thinking about work while at home
- voice tremor
- withdrawing from supportive relationships.

The Depression Checklist

Depression may be reactive, and may be caused by high levels of long-term stress; by the type of life crises described on pages 11–12; or simply by a sense of failure at underachievement. The boundaries between long periods of unhappiness, exhaustion, poor-quality sleep, worry and feeling out of control are often blurred.

Endogenous depression is another matter, however, as it is chemical in origin, and less related to day-to-day events and stress.

One of the problems with depression is that it may creep up on you so slowly and insidiously, that you don't even realise you are depressed. By that stage, the downward spiral of depression and its knock-on effects on energy levels, job performance, ability to communicate with colleagues, family and friends and overall quality of life may be almost catastrophic.

A high proportion of people who consult a GP for sleeping problems, or aches and pains of unknown origin, weight loss/gain, or chronic tiredness, are suffering from depression, but simply don't realise it. The great pity is that they don't seek help sooner, because in terms of alleviating severe symptoms, modern anti-depressants really work.

Recognising that you have a problem, and knowing how and where to get help, is the key to starting to get that problem under control. You can then seek psychotherapy or counselling, or take some other course of personal action. The checklist below may be the first step in that process.

If you experience four or more of the following symptoms for more than two weeks, you probably have depression and should consult your GP for help.

1 Are you feeling persistently sad, anxious, or do you have an empty feeling?
2 Are you tired, or slowed down, despite rest?

3 Have you lost interest in food, sex or work?

4 Are you waking during the night, or too early in the morning, or having trouble getting to sleep?

5 Have you lost weight (without dieting), or gained weight?

6 Are you having difficulty thinking, remembering, or making decisions?

7 Are you feeling guilty or worthless?

8 Have you been having thoughts of death or suicide?

9 Do you have aches or pains without a physical cause?

Usually, but not always, problems such as difficulty getting off to sleep, early morning waking or oversleeping (say for nine/ten hours or more), will go hand in hand with depression. It is, however, possible to be severely depressed but not have any of these particular sleeping problems.

CHAPTER 5

Stress Management

God grant me the serenity to accept the things I cannot
change, the courage to change the things I can and the
wisdom to know the difference.

The Serenity Prayer

I f the Serenity Prayer is the heart and philosophy of stress
management, then the practical and essential tools for seeing
the task through are:

◆ increasing self-awareness at multiple levels (cognitive)
◆ choosing to de-stress (behavioural)
◆ being pro-active about self-care (physical).

Control is one of the keys to managing stress. Orla O'Neill is
the Director of the Dublin County Stress Clinic. She says that
attaining and maintaining control inevitably involves incorpor-
ating cognitive, behavioural and physical changes into our lives.
There are no quick fixes.

Flexible cognition is one of the most powerful psychological skills anyone can have. It creates an opportunity to view
life through a different lens. Once you have got into the way of
focusing cognition, you won't turn the clock back, she says.

Emotional and Life Style Audit

The first step in this cognitive process is to carry out a kind of
emotional and life style audit on yourself. This necessitates asking

some searching and fundamental questions. It requires taking a step back from life to reflect — a holiday or a weekend break may be all the time that's required to do the trick. But if you cannot manage the process by yourself, enlist the help of a GP, your partner, good friend, counsellor, psychologist or psychiatrist.

Orla O'Neill recommends asking yourself a series of questions such as:

1 What are my core beliefs and values?
2 What are the most important things in my life right now — religion, love, health, money, work, family, relationships, hobbies, rest, relaxation, recreation time or lack of it?
3 What are my dreams? My ambitions?
4 What makes me happy/gives me the greatest sense of fulfilment?
5 What are my strengths and weaknesses?
6 What am I expecting of myself, and what can I actually do?
7 Do I know my personality type?
8 Do I know what my personal anchor points are in life?
9 If I were to look back on my life at the age of sixty-five, what are the things I would have liked to achieve? What would I feel good about?
10 Is my life balanced? Or am I defined predominantly by a particular area — money, work, relationships?

The second step involves looking at your current behaviour to see how everything is panning out. The purpose of this part of the exercise is to identify where the gaps lie between core values, priorities and specific aspirations, and current life style/ activities. In other words, are you leading the kind of life you *want* to lead?

The key questions are along the lines of:

Family Do I enjoy being with my family — partner, parents, siblings or children? Do I want a child? More children?

Health Am I as healthy as I should be? Do I suffer from any of the symptoms listed on page 21?

Life plan Do I know where I want to be in five/ten/twenty years' time? Do I have specific plans for career, family, children, self-development? Have I specific, but as yet unfulfilled, ambitions?

Love Do I feel loved? Am I happy with my partner? Am I searching for something better? Have I lost someone or something I love?

Money How do I rate job satisfaction compared to money? How much money do I really need to live? What, if any, is the shortfall? Could I get by on less? Am I putting myself under financial pressure for the sake of appearances, or status? Could I benefit from the services of a financial advisor?

Recreation How much time do I schedule myself every week for socialising, exercising, being with the people who matter to me? What are my main hobbies and interests, and how much time am I devoting to them each week? How much fun is there in my life? Do I have the kind of social life I really want, and with the kind of people who really interest me?

Relationships Are most of my relationships supportive? If not, which ones are giving me grief? Do I find myself saying 'yes' frequently when I'd rather say 'no'?

Religion What role does religion play in my life? Is it one of my anchor points?

Rest How much rest am I getting — sleep, breaks, time to do nothing, holidays?

Time Do I have enough time to do all the things I want and need to do? Or am I constantly behind schedule, over-extended?

Work If I am not working, do I need/want a job? If working, does the job I have suit me? Do I enjoy it? Are any of my work colleagues getting at me? Am I spending the right amount of time working? Have I got the requisite skills and training for my job, or should I be considering further training/self-development? Another career altogether? Become self-employed? Job share?

The third step is to look at the physical and self-care aspects of your life. The more physically fit you are, the quicker you will unwind after stress. Self-care in all its manifestations is not an indulgence, it's a necessity.

A number of further questions can be asked now, first on the subject of mental health:

1 How would I rate my level of self-esteem currently?
2 Do I know how to use supportive self-talk?
3 What are my favourite treats when I am under stress — massage, aromatherapy, cinema, holiday, taking a weekend break, having a facial or a hairdo, slap-up meal, reading a novel, phoning friends, taking a long bath, unplugging the phone?
4 Do I have anchors of predictability in my life, in terms of a regular life style?
5 Do I have people who will look after me when the going gets tough? If so, who are they? Do I feel supported generally?
6 Am I mentally stimulated? Do I feel the need to learn and experience a range of new things?
7 Am I good at communicating needs, wants and opinions with work colleagues? Children? Parents?
8 Do I negotiate what I want with friends?
9 Do I get depressed? Tired?

A number of other questions arise, concerning your general physical health:

1 How many of the life event crises listed on pages 11–12 apply to my life in the last two years?
2 If my score is high, what self-care adjustments have I made to take account of that?

3 How does my diet compare with the healthy guidelines set out on page 69?

4 When did I last have a check-up? Visit the dentist?

5 How many hours every week do I give to premeditated self-care (exercise, yoga, the Alexander Technique, meditation, deep relaxation, massage, a heart-to-heart talk with someone whose opinion I value?)

6 Does my work create physical or emotional stress?

7 How much am I smoking? Drinking?

Other questions relate to relaxation:

1 Do I have specific breathing, or deep relaxation, techniques for coping with stressful situations? To minimise/prevent a stress response?

2 Do I have a regular aerobic exercise regime, or do I regard relaxation as something merely for whatever time — if any — is left over after work.

3 When was the last time I had a really good laugh?

A Self-Esteem Diary

Apart from damage to physical health, damage to self-esteem is probably one of the first casualties of negative stress. When stressed, you tend to diminish the positive and over-emphasise the problematic, often underestimating your achievements and thus undermining your self-confidence. A useful tactic for gaining a more realistic assessment of your abilities and achievements is to keep a self-esteem diary. Check whether you operate a double standard, in terms of how you compare yourself with other people. This involves a very simple process. Each day, pick out some positive achievements, however small. Select three things, from examples such as:

◆ I smiled at somebody

- ◆ I paid someone a compliment
- ◆ I managed not to lose my patience in a difficult situation
- ◆ I did three tasks I've been putting off
- ◆ I walked somewhere instead of taking the car
- ◆ I helped the kids with their homework
- ◆ I did an errand for a neighbour
- ◆ I took a formal lunch break, rather than having a sandwich at my desk as usual.

Maintain this routine for four or five days. Then, on day five, say, start a second column on the same page; beside the three small daily achievements, list one *important* achievement. This can have occurred at any time in your life, and may include:

- ◆ I got married and reared children
- ◆ I'm *still* married
- ◆ I learned a musical instrument at school
- ◆ I learned how to drive/cook/fly/use a computer
- ◆ I passed an exam
- ◆ I got a place in university
- ◆ I got the job I wanted
- ◆ I bought my own home
- ◆ I was a member of the school basketball team
- ◆ I learned to paint.

This list-making process may seem contrived, but it is very helpful, because it completely changes attitude. If you are heading for trouble as a result of coping with current difficulties, this process will reframe your thinking, by challenging automatic thoughts — invariably negative ones.

Dealing with Difficult People

The do's and don'ts of dealing with difficult people is a huge subject. Because giving detailed descriptions and prescriptions is not possible within the confines of one chapter in a short book, this chapter focuses on general principles and guidelines, covering workplace stress creators predominantly. The area of living with difficult people is dealt with briefly in the latter section.

Encountering people with challenging personalities, or actual personality disorders, in the workplace is by no means unusual, and can be very stressful. Having a personality disorder does not necessarily mean these people are psychiatrically disturbed, in the sense of being unable to function. They *do* function, but usually at the price of stressing their colleagues and driving them to despair.

At one end of the spectrum, there's the problem of having to cope with people with, for example, narcissistic personality traits. Such people are terrible to work with. They tend to be pretty hysterical; they personalise everything; they find it hard to believe that the world does not revolve around them; and they can get hurt at the least provocation.

If this narcissistic personality type is at the 'exotic' end of the communications management spectrum, then the following are the more 'common or garden' varieties of stress-creating personalities that you are likely to come across in the workplace.

The Non-Assertive Person

This type of person is passive, and typically:

◆ avoids taking responsibility for anything
◆ behaves like a doormat
◆ feels like a victim
◆ finds it hard to make decisions
◆ is inhibited
◆ very often self-pitying
◆ puts themselves down.

If given a huge task, won't complain, but will probably go away and virtually have a nervous collapse from worry.

The Aggressive Person

This person is typically:

♦ demanding
♦ disempowering
♦ loud
♦ puts others down
♦ very often blaming.

If given a major task, will probably do something inappropriate.

The Indirect Aggressive Person

This person typically:

♦ avoids direct confrontation, but 'comes in the back door'
♦ blames everybody but themselves
♦ is vengeful
♦ makes others feel guilty
♦ manipulates
♦ plays one person off against another.

If given a huge task, will start wondering who they can blame.

The Assertive Person

By contrast with all of the above, this type:

♦ accepts their own limitations but struggles to improve
♦ accepts responsibility for their actions
♦ believes it is OK to make mistakes
♦ believes it is OK to ask for thinking time when they don't know the answer to something
♦ builds more honest, open relationships and gets more of what they want
♦ feels good about themselves

- is clear, direct and honest
- is confident, but can still feel scared or unhappy about confronting difficult situations
- is a good negotiator, and will actively go for win-win situations
- is not afraid of compromise, and takes a realistic view of the world
- recognises that there is no such thing as perfection
- respects themselves, as well as other people
- will allow themselves to enjoy their success
- will ask for help if they cannot do something
- will use a lot of 'I' statements, such as 'I would like ...'; 'I want ...'

If given a huge task, will ask for extra time to complete it.

Asserting yourself in the workplace, as opposed to being aggressive, can help communication and reduce your stress levels. Assertive people are healthy. They are the sort of people you like to be around, because you know where you stand with them. You may disagree with them, but you know they are fair.

In terms of both maintaining healthy relationships and managing difficult people, assertive behaviour works. In fact, assertiveness and communications skills are the key to successful stress management.

The central manifestations of appropriate assertive behaviour are:

- Keeping it Short and Simple (KISS); if you do this, you are far less likely to be side-tracked
- standing or sitting in a very open way
- maintaining good eye contact, and the most relaxed facial expression possible
- maintaining physical distance
- speaking clearly, but not raising your voice.

Gladeana McMahon is a psychotherapist and Co-Director of Problem Focused Psychotherapy Training at the Centre for Stress Management in London. She lists a number of strategies for dealing with confrontations/difficult situations.

The Three-Step Model

Using this model, an assertive person will begin a confrontation or difficult conversation by:

1 Acknowledging something on behalf of the other person, along the lines of 'I understand you might be upset with me about ...'
2 Adding a linking thought, like 'However, I really feel ...'
3 Finishing with 'and ...', detailing a specific new suggestion or compromise.

An assertive person looks for a 'win win' outcome wherever possible.

The Broken Record

This type of communication is designed to prevent somebody taking you off the point. The idea is to repeat the *essence* of what you've had to say, in as many different ways as you can, while remaining on the point. The trick is not to sound like a parrot, because you could inadvertently let slip 'but I already said that to you'.

You should preface your interjections with something like 'I appreciate that. However, as I said earlier ...,' or 'I can hear how upset you are. However ...,' always returning to the essence of your point of view.

Fogging

Fogging is very good for defusing difficult, aggressive people. Using this tactic, you agree with *part* of their complaint: 'Yes, I know I can be a bit difficult sometimes.'

Learning the Skills

Nobody learns to become assertive overnight. First, you must identify where your weaknesses are, and then decide how to get help — by reading a book, going to an assertiveness class, learning new communication skills. The important thing to remember about assertiveness skills is that acquiring them is a bit like learning to drive: it is difficult to co-ordinate all the elements at first, but it becomes automatic with practice. It's essential to keep chipping away and practising all the time.

One of the acid tests of how well you are doing is how you cope with a bully. Any one of the main personality types (non-assertive, aggressive or indirectly aggressive) can manifest as a bully. Traits common to all three types may include feeling out of control, insecure, low in self-esteem or frustrated.

It is essential to stand up to bullies. An assertive person will always try to sort out a problem either by considering formal grievance channels, or by responding to a distressing encounter with a statement like, 'If you continue to shout at me in this way, I shall have to consider what action to take next.'

The Golden Rules — a Summary

Don't set yourself up to fail. Rate the situations you would like to be more assertive in on a scale of zero to eight in terms of degree of difficulty. Start with something around a four or five. Starting with an eight could mean setting yourself up to fail. Dealing with lesser problems just ensures greater success. Then take the following steps.

Analyse your situation. How much is me? How much is the other person? What is going on at the moment?

Decide what you're going to do about it. Go out and learn assertiveness skills? Sit down and plan what you're going to say to the boss/office bully tomorrow?

Act on it. Do something — don't sit around griping. Now that you've analysed your situation, and decided what you need to do, line up your resources and now *go do it*!

A Final Word — At Home, or With Your Partner

The skills recommended for dealing with difficult people at work can be used to handle personal relationships of any kind. As with the workplace scenario, the most important thing to remember is that assertiveness skills permeate the whole of your life. Here are some common scenarios and suggestions on how to handle various types of personal situations in the least stress inducing way.

1   *Dealing with the sulker* Sulky behaviour is often displayed by indirectly aggressive personality types. If not handled properly, it can be very intimidating. The same types of techniques you would use with children can be very helpful: in other words reward good and ignore bad behaviour. It is not helpful to appease the sulker. Nor should you mirror their own behaviour and treat like with like.

The first approach is to try and elicit the ostensible cause of the upset. If that fails, the second approach could be along the lines of:

It seems as if there's something you're not happy about. I have tried to talk to you about this. However, it seems you don't want to talk to me at the moment. I'm not prepared to be punished for something, when I know neither the reason nor the cause. What I'm going to do is leave you with your feelings, and I hope at some point in the future you'll be able to come and talk to me.

In the meantime, it is vitally important that the non-sulker gets on with planned activities, ignoring the unwanted behaviour.

2 *Bringing things to a head* It is a fine distinction, but bringing things to a head is not the same as making them worse.
   What *is* worse is colluding with a difficult person and
   trying to appease them. In that instance, all you're actually
   doing is perpetuating unhealthy, maladaptive behaviour.

That said, most people are not comfortable with the idea of
confronting bad behaviour, because it may mean creating an
argument. However, bringing things to a head is often the
healthiest option. Letting issues fester under the surface is not.
If a partnership cannot stand the kind of scrutiny that ensues
from a major discussion about particular difficulties, then
you're probably in the wrong relationship. Ultimately, you may
have to decide whether to stay in it or simply move on.

3 *Co-dependent no more* Your self-esteem should never be
   dependent on anyone else. If you're living with a difficult
   person, it is vitally important to try and step back from
   their behaviour. If you find yourself constantly adapting to
   what they want and need, then you're living your life in a
   co-dependent and, ultimately stressful, way.

If you choose to continue your relationship with a difficult
person, it is important to look after yourself. No-one can make
anyone change. They have to want to do that themselves. Make
sure you have as full a life as possible. Take breaks, meet friends
and rest. Very often when a co-dependent partner starts living
their own life, it forces the difficult person to confront their
behaviour. Do not expect this to happen overnight, as it takes
time for the co-dependent person's new behaviour to establish
itself. The difficult person needs to realise that the changes are
here to stay.

CHAPTER 6

Stress Busters Round Up

The following is an eclectic mix of cognitive, behavioural and physical stress-prevention tips.

Cognitive

Narrow/negative thinking creates muscular tension and other autonomic responses. To prevent that kind of self-induced stress, monitor yourself for use of words indicating negative or rigid thinking. It only takes a few seconds for a thought, image or experience to create an alarm response, so avoid words such as, *should, must, have to, can't, always, owe and deserve* and *stupid*.

The more 'shoulds', 'musts' and 'oughts' you carry around with you, the more pressure you are putting on yourself, and the more likely you are to feel guilty. Try some opposites instead: *could, want to, don't want to, try to, often* and *clever*.

Create a Positive Environment

Practise giving and taking compliments. Create the most positive environment possible wherever you go. Practise smiling. If you're not already in the habit of giving people positive feedback, get into the swing of it now. Sincere compliments and a word of thanks will be appreciated, and will reap dividends from most people. Being overly flattering, or patronising, on the other hand, will almost certainly antagonise. There's a world of difference between the two.

Avoid people who put you down, blame you a lot, or generally give you grief. In work situations, avoid the trap of spending lunch breaks or other relaxation time moaning about work, colleagues or office politics.

See if you feel a sense of low self-esteem, or physical tension, after a period of being with certain people. Consider severing negative relationships if the situation is bad enough and you cannot change it. Key questions to ask yourself are: Does this person make my muscles tense? Or my heart pound? Give me a knot in my stomach? Make me sweat? Give me a headache? Make my hands and feet cold and clammy?

As well as keeping the kind of daily achievements journal mentioned above, keep a note of your thoughts on stressful situations and how you dealt with them. (The section on cognitive therapy on pages 107–9 explains how and why this process works.)

Write out the short-, medium- and long-term life goals you have identified from the life style audit on pages 26–30. Enter those in your daily journal fly-sheet, and on a card carried around in your wallet. Look at them from time to time — to refocus, revise and check off what's been achieved. Give yourself credit for completed efforts.

At least once a day ask yourself: What do I need to be doing to take care of myself right now? Breathing? Posture? Plans for exercise, recreation or relaxation?

The Importance of Control

Remember the point made earlier about how important a factor control is in the whole stress equation. In an ideal world, a feeling of power to exert control can go a long way towards helping stressful situations. It's often the main reason why people decide to become self-employed. The majority of people don't have the luxury of dictating their own agenda, however, so exerting power over people and situations isn't always possible. Controlling how you *respond* to people and situations *is* within your control, however.

Whenever you are faced with a work crisis or personal drama, ask yourself: Will this issue still be important in five or ten years' time?

Behavioural

Take regular breaks while carrying out a major piece of work — be it something like writing, or a more physical task like gardening, or cleaning. Indulge yourself with a few minutes' break (or better still ten minutes) to phone a friend or relative. Practise deep breathing, or stretching exercises. Do something pleasant — daydream, open a window for a breath of fresh air, or simply get up and move about. The benefits can be both physical and psychological. They may also help improve the quality of your concentration afterwards, and the resultant finished product.

The mind can only focus on problems for a limited amount of time. Play is as important as work, so try to spend at least half an hour every day having fun, doing non-problem solving activities (hobby, exercise, dancing, music) — with no inter-ruptions. Refuse unreasonable requests and demands — say 'I don't know', and 'I don't really care', when you don't.

Exercise and Relaxation

Make sure you have some short exercise periods in your day, every day. Use lunch hours to take a walk, get some fresh air. Park the car a bit further away from your destination than necessary, and walk the rest of the way. Keep a pair of trainers in the boot for those times when you get an opportunity to take a longer walk.

Make deep relaxation breathing part of your everyday routine. Practise it while standing in a queue; as you're stuck in traffic; sitting in the doctor's waiting room; before you take or make a telephone call; or while waiting for a meeting. See pages 93–4 for tips on how to breathe correctly.

Reducing Stress at Work and at Home

Create stress-free havens and stability zone reminders in your immediate workplace surroundings. Keep photographs of family, your favourite place, or a holiday postcard in a prominent place on your office desk, or in the kitchen.

Get into the habit of writing down good ideas — career related, children related, household management related, whatever. Otherwise they may get lost, like good pens! And on the subject of pens, keep some beside the telephone, tied on a string if necessary. Likewise a supply of scrap paper or 'Post Its' for notes, messages or shopping lists.

To avoid being overcome by that doormat feeling, agree some division of labour for household tasks. Rotate those tasks weekly, so that nobody can complain that they're always stuck with the dirty/boring/tiring jobs. Stick up a rota sheet on the fridge, so that the shirkers can't pretend they don't know who's responsible for what.

Stress and interruptions impair digestion, so if you haven't got one already, consider buying an answering machine and turn it on during family meal times. Or simply take the phone off the hook. Outside meal times, get into the habit of using the sound of a phone ringing as the cue to stop, breathe and relax (try a shoulder shrug), before you answer it. Let it ring at least twice before you pick it up.

If you are having a meal alone, don't read or watch TV while eating. Eating is a worthwhile activity in its own right — you should be aware of flavours, portion sizes, colours and textures. Do not eat out of packets or tins. Be civilised! Put everything you eat on a plate — even if it's only biscuits, crackers or a piece of fruit. Always sit down when you are eating. Some researchers believe listening to fast music makes you eat faster. Presumably much depends on the type of music you're listening to. If in doubt, why not turn it off?

Tight clothes can make you uptight, so consider a change of wardrobe, if necessary.

If carrying out a list of chores or boring jobs, make a contract with yourself to do something rewarding, pleasant or self-indulgent each time you complete one of those tasks. If you take on a major painting or gardening job, it's even more important to take restorative breaks. To make the most of your energy and enthusiasm levels, make a contract with yourself to spend no more than a certain number of hours, or minutes, on hard tasks. Allow for tidying and clearing up time afterwards.

If you live in a two-storey house, make sure each trip gives a double return for the effort. Get into the habit of bringing something upstairs/downstairs with you each time. Double up on the boring stuff by doing something pleasant or rewarding at the same time — talk on the phone with friends while ironing; listen to a language or book tape while cooking or painting.

Consider getting a pet. Interacting with an animal can be relaxing. Choose carefully, making sure to pick a low mainten-ance variety if you're out working all day and have no one to feed and water it.

Structured Relaxation

Finally, make a music relaxation tape for those periods when you have time to yourself and want to unwind in a structured way. The following are some suggestions for a classical music selection:

- Beethoven, *Pastoral Symphony*
- Boccherini, *Cello Concerto in B* (Adagio)
- Debussy, *Danses Sacred and Profane*
- Glinka, *Life of the Tsar*
- Pachelbel, the *Canon*
- Ravi Shankar, *Meditative Music*

◆ Sibelius, *Swan of Tuonela*
◆ Vivaldi, *The Four Seasons*

I can also recommend the works of contemporary US composer and musician Steve Halpern. Choose from a huge list of suitable recordings, far too long to enumerate here.

Finally, there's the recently released *8 Meditations for Optimum Health*, by Dr Andrew Weil. On this CD, Dr Weil's speaking voice is combined with music that has been created to have specific effects on the nervous system through the use of psycho-acoustics.

Dr Stephen Palmer, Director of the Centre for Stress Management in London, says he always advises students to listen to Mozart when studying. Some Japanese studies indicate that this improves IQ on a temporary basis. That knowledge in itself may help reduce stress!

An Extra Tip

First published in 1975, Shirley Conran's book *Superwoman* is still a terrific read. Obligatory for both women and men, it is a treasure trove of drudgery-reducing and time-saving tips, particularly for anyone juggling the obligations of family life as well as working outside the home.

Physical

You need to learn to recognise the signs of stress; these include shallow breathing, increased heart rate, headache, cold hands and feet, dry mouth and muscle tension. Breathe, and try to loosen up whenever you feel them coming on. A combination of diaphragmatic breathing and half a dozen shoulder shrugs (yes, literally!) are very effective. Aerobic exercise is the best way to eliminate stressful chemicals if you have been exposed to a stressful situation and need to recover quickly.

If you're sitting at a computer, or at a desk, keep checking on your posture and realign yourself to be more comfortable. Try not to strain your neck and back. Turn your whole body towards the object of your attention, rather than just your head. Do shoulder shrugs every hour or so. Stop for three to four minutes every half hour to stretch your muscles and maintain proper circulation.

Stressful life style or not, regular exercise is extremely important. Specific directives on what types of exercise are best, and how much to take, are set out in Chapter 8. If formal exercise or sport are ruled out for you, then try walking. The minimum recommendation for fitness is walking for thirty minutes, or more, at least four times a week.

It is also important to have a balanced diet. See Chapter 9 for specific tips on nutrition and vitamin/mineral supplements.

Try to keep regular sleep cycles, with no more than one hour variation each night. At weekends, a little more latitude is OK, but any variation of more than two hours oversleeping may cause Sunday Night Insomnia. (See *Sleep: The CommonSense Approach* for detailed information on how to get good sleep.)

Avoiding Stimulants

If you're already stressed, keep your coffee consumption as low as possible. If you're susceptible to the effects of caffeine, don't consume coffee or drinks containing caffeine, such as colas or hot chocolate, for four to six hours before bedtime. They may interfere with sleep, and insufficient sleep may stress you even further. See pages 73–4 for other comments and cautions about coffee consumption.

Use alcohol sparingly in times of stress. It is a stimulant, not a sedative, and is no friend to someone in difficulty. At the very time when you may need to think clearly and make rational decisions, alcohol will create precisely the opposite effect. It also destroys B complex vitamins. See page 74 for cautions/recommendations on alcohol consumption.

Don't use alcohol as a means of getting to sleep either. Like some sleeping pills, alcohol depresses the brain systems that control wakefulness. As its effects wear off, a wake rebound reaction occurs. This causes restlessness and fragmented sleep. It also increases the chances of waking up in the middle of a dream. In terms of social drinking, it is important to remember that the body takes one hour to metabolise each unit of alcohol. So four drinks consumed in the pub before bedtime equals four hours of recovery time.

It may be a natural reaction to reach for a cigarette during times of stress, but in fact it's probably the worst thing you could do to exacerbate the problem. Quite apart from the damage cigarettes do to the lungs and other organs, nicotine creates an almost immediate effect by increasing the heart rate — thereby generating even further stress.

Travelling is in itself stressful. To help yourself as much as you can, when making airline bookings ask for an aisle seat so that you can stretch your legs, or get up to walk around without disturbing fellow passengers.

And So To Bed ...

Finally, if you're trying to unwind after a tough day, bestselling writer and health specialist Leslie Kenton recommends a lukewarm bath, submerging yourself as much as possible for ten minutes. Then, wrapping a towel around you just long enough to get rid of the drips, pop into bed immediately. Lukewarm water is the most relaxing of all temperatures on the body. A hot bath before bed is a mistake — it is far too stimulating to the heart, and gets your motor running.

CHAPTER 7

Time Management — Practical Tips

I f you don't know where you're heading, you're likely to end up somewhere else.

This statement may seem like a long way from time management but, as will be clear from the previous pages, lack of clear goals, direction and a feeling of control are often a major source of stress, and make time management an aspiration rather than a reality. There are any number of time management courses. All will teach you that real time management is focused on *results*, not activity, not busyness.

To start the process of identifying clear goals and direction, begin by looking at a three- , six- or twelve-month time frame. Whatever goals list you devise should be for now and the foreseeable future, not for the rest of your life, because priorities and circumstances may evolve or change.

If you have a hectic life style, use unproductive time to begin this process — while vacuuming, painting, ironing, weeding the garden, commuting, waiting for a meeting to start; during a meeting if it's boring you to death; on the telephone waiting to be connected to someone you're calling. The goals list should relate to key areas in your life. They must be:

◆ a mix of short, medium and long term (days/weeks, months and years)

- realistic rather than aspirational — wishful thinking has no role in this exercise
- self-created, *not* targets imposed by someone else
- specific and quantifiable (in terms of numbers, money, increases/decreases)
- time-based, and have a particular deadline identified for achieving them
- tough and clear.

When completed, the main elements of a list might look something along the lines of the following:

Job Grow the business by twenty per cent within two years; take one Friday off every month from now on; move my home nearer work within the next year; train a staff member to take on extra responsibilities by November; delegate certain responsibilities/activities to someone else within the next six months; investigate the possibility of working from home some of the time by May; do a major tidy-up of my desk tomorrow.

Money Make or borrow £X by year end to move house/buy a new car/upgrade equipment; invest in a pension plan; hire home help; take more holidays and breaks.

Family/relationships Be home early enough to read the children a story two nights a week; have a romantic evening with my partner one night a week; invite friends to dinner once a month; devote a certain amount of time to an elderly relative once a week for the next six months; go hiking with the family next Sunday.

Hobbies and interests Organise a game of golf/tennis/squash once a week; start an evening course; see a play/film/show once a fortnight; read a bestselling book every month.

Self-care Join a yoga class next month; go for a swim on the way home from work three times a week; meditate for twenty minutes twice a day; have a massage/facial once a month; visit the dentist every six months.

As already described in Chapter 6, Stress Busters Round Up, when you have identified your specific goals, commit them to your diary, or bedside daily journal, if you've started keeping one. You should make a habit of reviewing the list regularly, to see if you're on target time wise, and to cross off anything you've achieved.

How Much is your Work Time Worth?

Now that you have established your goals, your next step should be to create a pecking order of priorities. Working out how much your time costs concentrates the mind wonderfully. If you're self-employed, out of 365 days every year, you have about 230 billable productive days available, after you have allowed for holidays and weekends. But no allowances there, obviously, for illness, pregnancy, paternity leave, child-care demands or other unforeseen eventualities.

Add the total costs of salary, taxes, overheads, professional fees, administrative support and equipment. Divide those costs by 230, and then again by eight, to get your hourly rate per working day.

By now you should have a whole new perspective on how much your work time is *really* worth. If you have a permanent and pensionable job, go through the same exercise. The details will differ, but the principle is the same. Keep that hourly/daily rate in mind whenever you're asked to travel somewhere, take on a new task, attend a meeting, join a committee, whatever.

How do you Spend your Day?

If you're currently having problems managing your working time, keep an activity log for a few days. Make a note of every single activity, from the moment you wake up. Include commuting time, all telephone calls, making tea, chatting to colleagues, dealing with post — everything.

Make sure you also keep a log of your energy peaks and valleys. If you're a lark, morning may be your most productive and creative time. This, therefore, is when you should carry out the most intellectually or emotionally demanding tasks. If you're an owl, productivity may increase as the day wears on, so evenings might be your best time for writing or strategic thinking work.

Mid-afternoon may be a valley time for both owls and larks, however. During the 2.30 to 4.30 p.m. time frame, the brain works more sluggishly. Mid-afternoon dip is extremely common, and is linked to our circadian rhythm cycle. Circadian rhythms also have a bearing on other functions, such as digestion. Digestion is optimum in the morning and at mid-day. If you follow a three-meals-a-day routine, have your biggest meal of the day then.

Isolate the Important

Next, examine the daily logs. Tick off which of the really important, as opposed to urgent, things got done. Compare that with how much time was spent dealing with other tasks. Differentiate between the results you achieved in those days and the tasks you completed. Compare the results with your key goals. See how big the gap is, and try to analyse where time got wasted, why and by whom. If the results don't look too good, you need help.

Stress Busting Equipment

If you can afford it, take one or two days off to do a time management course. If that's not an option, buy a personal organiser. And if that's not an option, a simple notepad will do. Enter your key goals, and devise an action plan for high pay-off tasks — in other words, *important* not *urgent* ones. As you commit to entering a date, keep asking yourself: Is this realistic, achievable?

In making plans and commitments, bear in mind Pareto's Principle, or the eighty/twenty rule. The basis of this rule is that, typically, eighty per cent of unfocused effort generates only twenty per cent of results. The remaining eighty per cent of results are achieved with just twenty per cent exertion.

Information Overload

In a recent survey carried out by Reuters Business Information, of 1,300 managers in the UK half reported that they were suffering from information overload. So bad was the problem of coping with reports, correspondence, e-mail, voice mail, phone and fax messages, it was causing both major job stress and affecting their home life.

The industrialised world is already suffering from information overload. For example, in a recent *Sunday Times* article, it was stated that a copy of a weekday edition of *The New York Times* contains more information than the average person living in seventeenth-century Britain would have come across in their entire *lifetime*. The same article also states that more information was produced between 1967 and 1997 than in the previous 5,000 years. Every twenty-four hours, another twenty million words of technical information are being produced.

If you're at the receiving end of a flood of material, consider Pareto's Principle. If you take the view that twenty per cent of the material that passes your way is worthwhile reading, could you get away with skimming the rest? This is just as true of unsolicited material that comes in through your letterbox. Learn to be ruthless with junk mail. Dump it. Better still, do something about blocking it at the source of origin. The Consumers' Association can tell you if there is a direct mail association in your area. That association may, in turn, arrange to have your name removed from companies' personalised mailing lists.

De-Stressing Work Time
Step 1: The Action Plan

Trying to carry around lists of projects to tackle and tasks to complete in your head (as opposed to committing them to paper), is a recipe for creating a mantle of unnecessary stress and worry. Writing prioritised lists and action plans is the first step on the road to de-stressing your working time. It really is effective.

For maximum return, you must produce an action plan for the following day the evening before. That plan must relate to how much uncommitted time you have available that day — there is no point overloading yourself. Restrict it to about fifteen tasks, and don't spend more than fifteen minutes working on it.

Lay the action plan/agenda out on the blank page opposite your diary page for the following day, and keep the diary pages for appointments only.

Before you fill in any action point, ask yourself if that task could be done equally well by somebody else, whose time is less valuable and who is available. If yes, then don't take it on yourself. *Delegate it* — even if you could do it better.

Don't make a random action list. If you have a number of projects on the go, create a box, or a heading for each. List them in some kind of pecking order — how much they are worth to you; how difficult they are; whether they are a possible source of new opportunities; whether your relationship with them is a bit wobbly, for example.

Into that pecking order goes the list of important tasks you *must* do next day. List these in descending order of priority. That way, the most important things should get done first. Niggly things can afford to linger at the bottom of the list until they get done, or fall off altogether (either because they've already gone out of date, or weren't important in the first place). Select from:

- major tasks to be done that day (remembering to put a *realistic* time estimate beside each one)
- list of key telephone calls in order of priority
- list of people to chase/nag
- major administrative or household management tasks
- former friends/contacts to touch base with, brain storm, keep abreast of news in the industry and business developments, marketing, or just plain old networking at coffee mornings, parent teacher associations, support groups or social clubs
- other tasks that don't fall into any of these categories.

At the bottom of every daily action sheet, leave a few lines for filling in chores/tasks relating to your personal life and self-care.

The most important thing about this time management and activity planning process is that you shouldn't permit anything other than crises to allow you deviate from your action list for the next day.

If, after all this, you have underestimated timing, because interruptions or people demands prevented you getting through the list, transfer the action points to the following day's sheet *until they do get done*. If you fail to transfer them to the daily action sheet, there's a good chance they won't be done at all.

When making appointments, get into the habit of writing the telephone number of whoever you're meeting directly underneath. This is handy for all sorts of reasons — to say you've been delayed en route; or perhaps for quick verification calls afterwards.

Some experts recommend starting each day by doing one difficult task — a 'monkey off your back task' — like sending a refusal letter; making a regrets phone call; drafting a page or two of a tedious report; tackling some element of a major task for that day. One of the reasons for this is the psychological lift it gives you — a sense of virtue and of achievement, for having started a task you've been postponing.

Aim for the ultimate in time management — vow to handle every piece of paper only once. The rule is:

◆ deal with it
◆ delegate it
◆ dump it.

Or re-circulate the same piece of paper with your hand written reply.

Three final points in relation to planning your day's activities:

a) Take account of the high and low points of your daily energy levels. Don't put major tasks in your diary for low energy or high interruption periods of the day. Best of all, combine high energy with low interruption, for example, when the phones are quiet.
b) Resist the temptation to do small/unimportant stuff at the high points of your daily energy cycle.
c) Take time to regularly review whether/how long it's taking to get through your lists. If items regularly roll over for days or weeks on end, then you must do an audit to find out why the system is not working. Are you underestimating the time you had allocated to tasks? Is someone/something interrupting or distracting you? Are machines/other resources letting you down? Is management/expert intervention needed? Are you not being ruthless enough with your time? Have you said 'yes' to new things in the meantime?

Step 2: Managing the Phone

Learn to manage everything to do with the telephone better. Where possible, initiate calls rather than accept them. Not only is it a better use of your time, but it may also give you a psychological and tactical advantage. Always have a clear idea of what the objective of the call is. Why am I doing this? What do I hope to achieve? Make a checklist of points to be communicated so that you get best use out of the call.

Get into the habit of timing calls, or at least know how long they are lasting. Maybe keep an egg timer by the phone, so that you make calls lasting three minutes or less. Consider standing up while you're on the phone — you'll be less likely to waste time chatting. Some experts also say that you come across as more authoritative if you're standing — something to do with voice projection and the lungs.

If you know that the person you're calling tends to be long-winded, arrange to be interrupted.

If you're pursuing a key decision maker, someone who is otherwise hard to pin down, work out when they are most likely to be at their desks rather than at meetings. For example, senior managers may start work at 7.30 a.m. (because it's good thinking/reading/writing time), and usually have no one to screen their calls at that hour. A security man, their only buffer, may put you straight through, unwittingly or otherwise.

You may also get that vital ten minutes of uninterrupted conversation with your GP, or your child's teacher, if you call just before their first patient/class.

When leaving messages, always give your phone number — it's more polite. In any event, you mustn't assume whoever you're phoning has it to hand. If they have to make several calls, then they'll also be less irritated if they don't have to go off searching for your number, and if they have some idea of what the call is about. Related to that, leave *specific* messages. If it's a simple request for information, then they can delegate someone to deal with your query, or leave a message with someone else if you call back later. That translates into a better use of everyone's time.

Get used to leaving clear, but *short* messages on answering machines and voice mails. Having to listen to long-winded messages can be stressful for someone with a busy schedule and workload. Like it or not, voice mail is becoming more common and it's here to stay. (In the US, it already accounts for eighty per cent of office telephone messages.)

Get to the point of a phone call quickly. Always assume whoever you're phoning is under time pressure, or suffering from information overload, even if they're not. Leave small talk until the end. Most people do the opposite. If you waste the first few minutes on small talk, the danger is whoever you're calling may be interrupted to take another call, or have to dash off for an appointment, so the opportunity to achieve your main purpose will be lost. If the call does get to the chit-chat stage, make sure to have a note of personal details about the call in front of you, such as spouse's name; health/hobbies/family details.

Consider making some calls just before lunch or going home time. The chances are that chatty types will be less likely to waste time if they have to be somewhere else shortly.

Experts say that a typical person wastes a fifth of every day trying to retrieve information. To cut down on time-wasting, clear out computer files regularly. Consider having just one ring binder file for each current project; use interleave sections to categorise information headings. Instead of major spring cleaning efforts once a year, do a little clearing out of desk and work-top clutter regularly. Staple relevant correspondence in chronological order. Don't paper clip documents, as this may result in inadvertent couplings of unrelated material!

Where possible, file material yourself as you go, and keep files within arm's reach. This is particularly helpful for retrieving information while on the telephone, or if you're about to dash off to a meeting. Use portable home file units for keeping household bills, warranty papers, equipment manuals and legal documents together. To cut down time spent searching for telephone numbers, group categories of things together according to whatever your key trigger words are. For example:

C for children/creche/childminders

E for emergency (alarm company, police station, spouse's direct line, automobile rescue, doctor-on-call, plumber)

F for family (sisters, brothers, parents, in-laws)

H for home (alarm company, builders, home help, painters, gardener, maintenance, gas company, central heating oil, insurance companies, cleaners, electrician)

M for anything medical (doctor/dentist/osteopath)

O for any kind of office/computer supplies and services

R for your favourite restaurants

S for children's schools.

Enter all telephone details in pencil — they may change.

For desk use, use a Rolodex. These store a huge amount of numbers and business cards, and the retrieval system is very fast.

Consider putting an extra long extension lead on your telephone so that you can move around the home, or office, while speaking on the telephone. This enables you to double up on tasks — feed the baby; turn down the radio; put on the toast; stir something on the cooker; reach for a journal; hand a colleague a document; fill your briefcase with materials before heading off for a meeting; unpack after a meeting.

Step 3: Schedule your Appointments

Get a reputation for being on time. If you are consistent about starting and finishing meetings on time, people are more likely to learn to respect or accommodate your time constraints. Group all meetings geographically — if you're calling the shots, and setting up various appointments in the same day. Be realistic about travelling and parking time. Cutting it fine and being late for an appointment puts you at a psychological disadvantage straightaway.

Arrange meetings for slightly unusual times, like 2.15, rather than 2.30 or 3 p.m. People will tend to respect that kind of odd start time. Some experts recommend setting extremely odd times, like 9.25, to create the impression that your time is really precious — but this in itself is quite precious!

Writing Tips

Rather than work at your desk, where you are likely to be interrupted, go elsewhere to write if you can. Try the organisation library, or an empty conference room. Specify when you'll be free. Ask someone to take messages, and brief them on the important calls. Then keep your word and return calls when you said you would. This creates confidence and credibility, relieves guilt — and, therefore, stress.

Start major writing jobs when your mind is clear, i.e. during high energy periods.

Don't try and do important writing jobs during peak telephone times.

A desk is a writing, not a storage space. Keep any writing environment free of clutter — have nothing on it, other than reference materials for the task in hand.

To avoid telephone shuffle, and time wasting at meetings, number pages (and paragraphs if necessary) of documents.

Make more use of conference calls to save time.

Use tape machines at briefing meetings. This allows you to concentrate on the content of what is being said, rather than having to take detailed notes. Use them for recording follow-up thoughts on meetings; action points; drafting the outline of a proposal document/letter.

Meeting Tips

All meetings should have a clear purpose, i.e. they should be designed to decide something, or impart information. They should have an agenda and a time limit. If possible, agree at the outset how long it is estimated to take.

In general, avoid breakfast/lunch/dinner meetings, unless you are hosting them on site. Otherwise they may eat a hole in your day.

The best time for a meeting may not necessarily be the time that *appears* to suit everyone. For example, meetings held very early in the morning, or on Saturdays and Sundays may, surprisingly, be a good idea. They are less inclined to be open ended. They should concentrate the mind more, because they are taking place in people's personal time.

If someone else has called the meeting and you cannot stay for the whole thing, announce your time constraints at the outset. The agenda can be rearranged to cover major points in which you have an involvement. That way, you avoid key decisions being made after you've left.

If hosting a meeting, avoid time wasting and the inter-ruptions of tea/coffee/water orders by having everything on the meeting table in advance, so people can help themselves. Use flasks.

If having a restaurant meeting with a client, and time con-straints/good service are an important factor, tip the waiter when you arrive, and explain that you need efficient service. If there are just two of you, book a table for three anyway — you're likely to get a bigger/better table.

Finally, it may also save time waiting for the bill if you leave your credit card at the desk when you arrive. Staff can then go ahead with processing it.

Always have your diary with you at meetings. If you can, encourage others to do the same. Use it conspicuously to minute decisions, commit to dates, etc.

Don't allow open-ended decisions. Always pin down action dates/deadlines — let it be seen that you're serious about them. People are more likely to stick to a deadline if they've set it/written it down themselves.

Noting action points in your diary at the time also saves you from having to go through meeting notes, or contact reports, back at the office. It is also less likely that relevant action points will be forgotten later.

Discourage the practice of calls being put through at meetings, unless earth-shatteringly important.

Make sure meeting rooms have appropriate materials and equipment (VCR, white board, flip charts, colour pens, etc.).

For internal meetings, use someone else's office. If they're being long-winded, it's much easier for you to make an excuse for escaping from their office, than it is to get them out of yours!

To discourage chatty people dropping into your office, leave a briefcase/stack of journals on your visitor's chair.

Time-Saving Tips

Procrastination takes time and mental energy, and is a serious distraction. Being nice is more time consuming than being honest. Get difficult phone calls/refusals/confrontations over and done with early in the day. Apart from taking a monkey off your back, it'll make you feel virtuous.

Painful decisions don't get any easier as time drags on. Get into the habit of saying 'no' when you mean 'no' — not 'maybe'.

After you've done a difficult task, reward yourself — with a cup of coffee, tackling something pleasant, phoning a friend.

Always carry small supplies of pens, envelopes, stamps and stationery in your bag/car for those 'dead times' spent sitting in traffic jams, waiting for people in pubs, restaurants, airport terminals or office reception areas.

Always carry some reading/writing work with you when you're out and about, for those occasions when you receive the gift of unexpected time.

Double up on the mundane/trivial stuff. Bin junk while waiting to be put through on the phone; hand write envelopes as someone is calling out the address; do almost anything that's legal and safe while driving (including listening to language, how-to or book tapes); review your action list for the day; write notes to friends ...

Don't get caught on the hop (and therefore have to drop something important as a result). Keep emergency supplies of birthday/thank you/get well/sympathy cards; home stationery; sewing repair kits; colds/flu/headache pills; or tights in a designated drawer.

Keep a certain amount of the above in your car also.

Hand-written rather than typed letters or notes are more appropriate for congratulations, thank you, sympathy or personal letters — and may save time.

If you regularly have to process lots of documentation, consider doing a speed reading course.

Keep a gift drawer at home — for the arrival of new babies; birthdays/emergencies; for when you've forgotten to buy a gift, or need a thank-you present.

Go *against* the flow if you find queuing and commuting stressful. For instance, go to work when people are sleeping, and come home when they're already at home, or still at work! Go shopping off-peak. Do bank/post office business at times when the queues are shorter, or there are no queues. Go to supermarkets at 8.30 a.m. or late in the evening. Apart from getting in and out of places faster, the chances are you'll get better service also.

Take holidays out of season, or at the beginning/end of season. As well as cheaper deals, you are likely to get better/ friendlier treatment.

Where services are equal — like dry cleaners, take-aways, video shops, gyms, hair dressers and banks, go where you can park outside (on your way to/from work). Keep some sort of geographical logic to all the services you use regularly.

Never go shopping without a list. For groceries, group them into logical categories, so that you don't waste time criss-crossing the supermarket.

Carry samples of colour swatches, actual garments, household furnishing measurements, children's/spouse's clothes sizes — for those occasions when you spot something unexpectedly.

Keep these details in the *Notes* section of your diary. Don't forget to take this information with you when travelling also.

Be ruthless about cleaning out clutter from cupboards, drawers, the garage, computer files, in-trays, bags and brief-cases regularly. This saves you time later when you're looking for a letter/document. Use unproductive time for these tasks.

Apply the same 'clear out' ruthlessness to wardrobes. Group clothes types together. Make sure you can find things quickly. Always have one totally accessorised and co-ordinated outfit dry-cleaned and ready for that unexpected client meet-ing/business trip /important social engagement.

Finally, clear your desk or work top at night. It's demoral-ising to start the day with the previous day's unfinished business staring at you.

Travelling

Advance book airline seats (if you're travelling business class). If a regular traveller, this reduces stress and time-wasting at check-in desks. Plan all your meetings geographically. Be realistic about the commuting time from venue to venue, otherwise you risk the snowball effect of being late for a series of appointments.

On long-haul flights, when you board the aircraft set your watch for the destination time. Then, arrange your eating, reading and dozing according to your watch. If you have an important meeting at the end of a flight, pack a spare change of underwear, shirt/blouse and some toiletries in a carry-on bag. Such foresight can do a great deal to relieve stress should your luggage go astray.

If you travel a lot, cut down on carrying unnecessary weight and packing time by having a separate kit of toiletries ready to go. Use plastic bottles to decant small quantities of cleansers, sham-poos, conditioners, medication, vitamin pills, whatever you need.

If travel is not part of your regular routine, keep a comprehensive travel checklist in your diary.

CHAPTER 8

Exercise

A ccording to Michael Hughes, a Californian psychologist and stress management trainer, the wear and tear on our bodies caused by typical office-based sedentary jobs is rarely considered to be stressful but can, in fact, be very much so.

Even the act of talking increases blood pressure, and can overwork both the cardiovascular system and throat area. Sitting for long periods of time can weaken and tighten muscles and joints throughout the body. Commuting to and from work can contribute to physical frustrations, and working more than eight hours a day means that even more time is needed to recuperate.

Michael Hughes says that an often underestimated and under-utilised remedy for this kind of sedentary stress — or indeed any kind of stress — is regular aerobic exercise, because it:

◆ burns up the residue of stress chemicals in the body
◆ increases metabolic efficiency
◆ increases oxygen flow
◆ strengthens muscles.

Some research findings indicate that people who are fit may be less physically reactive in certain stressful situations, and have a shorter recovery time.

The Body's Response to Stress
The body responds to stressful situations by releasing hormones into the bloodstream. As already described earlier in this book,

if the chemical onslaught is sufficiently severe, and continues for long enough, those hormones can eat away at the digestive tract and lungs, promoting certain types of ulcers and asthma.

Even short-term exposure to stress will leave a chemical imprint. Hormones may linger in muscle tissue for a long time after stressful situations, such as an aggravating telephone call, an argument with a family member over breakfast, or an altercation with another driver while commuting to work. Once aroused, the body may remain in a state of over-mobilisation (semi-arousal) long after its need for the automatic flight-or-fight response hormone, adrenaline, has passed. Unless you make a deliberate attempt to eliminate the adrenaline by using some combination of aerobic exercise followed by progressive relaxation, deep breathing, meditation or exercise, it will linger on.

The lingering effect of the adrenaline and the low-grade flight-or-fright response may then result in irritability, difficulty in concentrating and sleeping and, ultimately, lower perfomance all round. A stressed person with high arousal levels, who does not get their quota of regular aerobic exercise, stores that tension and stress chemical residue in their body until it either dissipates, or leads to stress and illness.

The Benefits of Aerobic Exercise

Aerobic exercise is one of the most time-efficient and effective ways of flushing residue out of the system, and relieving muscular tension. This is one reason why it is a powerful antidote against the effects of both long- and short-term stress.

Another reason it is a powerful weapon in anti-stress armoury is that even moderate exercise affects both brain and body functions. The body is, after all, primarily a pump. Exercise affects overall performance by improving the efficiency of the metabolic system, increasing the vital flow of nutrients throughout the body, increasing oxygen to the brain and altering mood positively.

As well as helping to reduce depression and contributing to weight loss, the other specific benefits of regular aerobic exercise include:

◆ helping to lower blood pressure
◆ increasing cardiovascular fitness
◆ improving muscular conditioning
◆ stimulating the release of endorphins — the brain's pleasure hormones — hence the feel-good factor.

Regular exercise increases energy and stamina, improves concentration, productivity and memory and overall mental performance. It is an excellent way of preparing the body for stress and performance — it makes daily life that bit easier. Aerobically fit individuals have improved self-esteem, and also tend to sleep better.

To qualify as proper aerobic exercise, the heart must pump at between sixty to seventy-five per cent of its maximum rate for an uninterrupted period — at least twenty to thirty minutes — three to five times a week. Depending on the individual, it may take a few minutes, or a great deal longer, to reach optimum heart rate, so that factor needs to be taken into account when determining the overall length of the exercise period.

The Heart Rate Calculation Formula

Take the number 220 and subtract your age. Multiply that figure by sixty per cent and seventy-five per cent respectively. For example, if you are thirty years of age, the formula would be:

◆ 220 - 30 = 190 multiplied by 60% = 114 training heart rate
◆ 190 multiplied by 75% = 142 training heart rate.

So during the requisite 20–30 minute exercise period, the heart rate should be between 114 and 142 beats a minute.

A note of warning, however. If you are obese (more than one-fifth over your ideal weight), or have any medical problems requiring regular medication, then you should check with your doctor before beginning any self-imposed aerobic exercise regime.

Some Further Advice

Forget the 1980s exercise concept of 'no pain, no gain'. It's certainly true for some aspects of training, but not necessarily healthy. It can also be dangerous. If you have had a primarily sedentary routine for a long time, are generally unfit and are aged over thirty-five, you should go for a medical check-up if you develop any of the following symptoms:

◆ dizziness or nausea
◆ exhaustion persists long after the exercise period
◆ feelings of tightness, pressure, or pains in chest, shoulder, arms or neck
◆ heart rate takes longer than fifteen minutes to slow down after exertion
◆ irregular heart rate, or skipped beats during exertion
◆ severe breathlessness, even after mild exertion.

If you have eschewed exercise for a long period, it is advisable to start by walking fifteen minutes every day for two to three weeks, before moving on to something more strenuous. You should then continue with that stretching routine as your aerobic exercise training begins.

Most exercise injuries happen because of rushing through the learning phase of new regimes, and because of too much straining. So, if you feel pain, you should stop and rest for a few days or longer.

All exercise should be preceded by a warm-up and cool-down period, lasting at least five to ten minutes. Remember that three to five times a week is optimum. If you exercise seven days a week, you are not giving the body time to repair and build stamina and strength. People who over-exercise are as prone to illness and injury as those who do nothing.

In addition, a proper exercise programme — one that combines aerobic fitness and flexibility training — should leave you feeling energetic, and ready to do battle with the stresses of everyday life.

Exercises for Dealing with Stress

Exercise that is relatively comfortable, convenient and non-competitive is more relaxing, and so has a particular relevance in the context of stress management. You should choose some-thing that uses the whole body, if possible. The most effective in terms of generating aerobic fitness, and therefore in terms of burning fat tissue, are:

- aerobics, or aqua aerobics, class
- cycling (outdoors, or using a stationary exercise bicycle)
- dancing (any type will help)
- gym work out
- rollerblading
- rowing (using gym equipment)
- running
- swimming
- skiing
- walking (preferably power walking).

Gardening and sports that are not played at a competitive level, and which have a stop/start motion, are not as effective in terms of achieving aerobic fitness. Sports like football, squash, tennis and golf will not necessarily maintain the heart rate at the requisite level. But being generally active will still go a long way towards maintaining health.

Where to Begin

If you haven't developed a life-long commitment to the benefits of regular exercise, then the likelihood is that your key motivators will be either inspiration or desperation. Maintaining that motivation is key to adhering to a regular exercise routine.

A successful start is important. Buy comfortable shoes and clothes; collect some information on local pools and gyms; schedule a short exercise period in your diary; buy an inexpensive exercise bicycle and use it while watching television or reading the paper.

Finding people to exercise with is one way to ensure that you stick to it. Picking something that's fun is another. But if you are confined to a solo routine for logistical, timing or other reasons, then exercising while listening to something interesting and engaging may do the trick. For instance, if you hate the pulsating music of a typical gym sound system, why not use a personal stereo to listen to a book cassette, language tape or classical music? You may become so engrossed in the tape that getting yourself off the treadmill may prove more difficult than you would ever have thought possible.

If neither a gym workout nor the aerobic exercises listed above appeal, then don't abandon the idea of exercise altogether. While less effective as a way of attaining and maintaining aerobic fitness, you will still derive a range of relaxation, recreation and other benefits by being generally active. Gardening, walking, hiking or an occasional game of tennis or golf will still generate some benefit, although they will not give you the health inoculation that regular aerobic exercise will.

CHAPTER 9

Nutrition and Diet

G ood diet and nutrition don't in themselves counter the effects of stress, but they do have a clear role in health maintenance. Sustaining the right kind of energy levels throughout the day, and keeping your weight at an appropriate level, are all part of stress management and the overall good-health equation.

US dietary experts have defined the optimal balance for good health as one combining a specific number of servings daily from each of the following six food groups:

◆ bread, cereals, rice, pastas, potatoes (6–11 servings)
◆ fats, sugars and sweets (sparingly)
◆ fruit (2–4 servings)
◆ milk, yoghurt, cheese (2–3 servings)
◆ meat, poultry, fish, dry beans, eggs and nuts (2–3 servings)
◆ vegetables (3–5 servings).

Dr Michael Gibney, Professor of Nutrition, Department of Clinical Medicine, Trinity College Dublin agrees with the fundamental principles of this kind of dietary regime. He has just two minor points of disagreement.

The first is the recommendation of a specific number of servings; Professor Gibney says that most people find it difficult to work out what exactly 'specific servings' means for them.

The second point of disagreement is with the idea that sugars should be used sparingly. Professor Gibney's personal view is that present levels of sugar consumption are not implicated in chronic disease; to suggest that we should restrict our intake would lead to higher fat diets (since dietary fat energy and sugar energy are inversely related). If the latter goes down, the former goes up, and that's not a wise strategy.

What Makes a Healthy Diet?

A healthy diet should be comprised predominantly of complex carbohydrates, such as pasta, potatoes, rice, breads and cereals. All the evidence now is that people should *not* be counting calories (and therefore reducing carbohydrates and sugars), but they should be monitoring fat intake and keeping this to a minimum.

Professor Gibney says that having a high carbohydrate, low-fat diet will reduce the risk of weight gain. One of the great misconceptions is that potatoes, pastas and other carbohydrates make you put on weight: they *don't*. Carbohydrates are not converted to fat in the body. They are used as fuel, and the body burns that fuel whenever energy is expended. Fat, on the other hand, is stored in the body, and is responsible for weight gain. The most efficient way to diet is to severely curtail fat intake. Overeating is much more difficult with a high carbohydrate diet, because carbohydrates are bulkier and have a much greater satiating effect on the brain.

He adds that consumption of fruit and vegetables in northern European countries is exactly half that of Mediterranean countries, and that most people could benefit from doubling their current intake.

Why Exercise?

Cardiovascular exercise is very important, and for reasons other than weight loss. In fact, the weight loss component of exercise is often grossly overstated. If you want to lose weight, exercise is a useful adjunct, because it makes you feel good, but it's not the most efficient way. The most efficient way is to severely curtail fat intake. If you run an additional ten kilometres once a week, for example, you burn 1,000 calories. Divided over seven days, that works out at about 142 calories — the equivalent of half a bag of crisps. Clearly, weight loss should not be the sole motivation driving exercise.

When to Eat

There seems to be no disagreement among the experts on the importance of eating a good breakfast. A combination of cereal, low-fat milk and sugar totalling 700 calories will be quite adequate, if the early morning rush doesn't allow for a cooked breakfast with fruit juice and all the trimmings.

After breakfast, the latest advice seems to be to continue through the day with frequent, but small, meals. One benefit of this over the traditional 'three square meals a day' regime is that people who favour more frequent but smaller meals tend to have slightly lower blood cholesterol. The principle underlying this recommendation is that each time we eat, we switch on the degradation of cholesterol in the liver. Obviously, the more often we eat, the more often we turn on that disposal mechanism.

In the context of a demanding, busy and stressful life style, it is also important to try and keep blood sugar levels consistent, and overall energy levels smooth. That is yet another reason for favouring short gaps between meals. Long gaps may mean either no fuel, or less fuel, and therefore less energy at the very times in a busy day when increased physical or mental performance may be required.

Vitamins, minerals and other supplements

If you are eating a balanced diet, then you shouldn't need to take dietary supplements or vitamins.

Restrained eating is, however, a major problem among women in particular, and where overall food intake is down, nutrient intake will be reduced pro-rata. Many high-achieving, successful career women compound the deficiency problem by combining a restrained eating pattern with a lot of exercise. In doing so, they are simply placing themselves in double jeopardy: twice the stress.

Such extreme cases aside, however, Professor Gibney is generally cautious about advising people with busy or stressful life styles to take vitamin and mineral supplements. He adds that the jury is almost certainly out on whether or not vitamin C has any prophylactic role in curing the common cold, for example. For women who fit the restrained eater/high exerciser profile, though, he says that the taking of dietary supplements and minerals may well be advisable.

Weight-obsessed teenage girls and restrained eaters in the under thirty-five age group, who restrict their consumption of dairy products, are putting themselves at risk of developing osteoporosis in later life. As a direct result of calcium deficiency brought about by their low dairy product consumption, osteoporosis is now a major problem in older women. Dairy produce is the preferred way to meet the body's calcium requirements, but a supplement may be indicated where dietary intake is insufficient, particularly among people who specific- ally avoid dairy products.

Restrained eating may also be responsible for iron insufficiency, something that affects one-third of all women, a percentage of whom are anaemic. If they become pregnant while anaemic, they will tend to have underweight babies. Research shows that how a child grows *in utero* at least partially determines their incidence of liver, heart and lung disease or diabetes in later life.

The other important point about diet and pregnancy is that all women of childbearing age — and particularly those who are planning a pregnancy — should take folic acid (one of the B vitamins) in supplement form *as a matter of course*. Folic acid plays a vital role in the development of a baby's neural tube. Dietary sources of this vitamin need to be supplemented.

If a mother's diet is deficient in folic acid, her chances of giving birth to a baby with spina bifida are increased. It is particularly important to take folic acid in supplement form in the peri-conceptual period (immediately before and after becoming pregnant). Unfortunately, despite the fact that spina bifida is a major public health problem, many women are unaware of, or choose to ignore, the folic acid message.

For men, taking folic acid may be important if their dietary intake is insufficient. New research indicates that folic acid may play a role in heart disease. As well as in supplement form, it is found in most fruits and vegetables, and in fortified foods such as many breakfast cereals.

Vitamin B12 injections may be recommended for elderly people suffering from depression and low vitamin B12 status. People over sixty have greater difficulty absorbing this vitamin, hence the requirement for supplementation.

Finally, it is important that people do not exceed the Recommended Daily Allowances (RDA) for the requisite vitamins and minerals. Ask your pharmacist or GP for advice on this. For women who are pregnant, lactating or suffering high menstrual loss, it is especially important to check your needs with a health professional.

Other Dietary Do's and Don'ts

Drink lots of water every day — six to eight glasses is about right, but you'll need more if you are engaged in strenuous exercise. Generally, the rule of thumb seems to be that if you're thirsty, the body is already dehydrated. So, avoid getting to this stage.

As stated earlier in the book, caffeine is a stimulant which increases the heart rate, and should therefore be avoided while dealing with stressful situations. It is also a diuretic: the effect can literally flush out the body's store of water-soluble B and C vitamins.

Because the body cannot tell the difference between real and imagined danger, it always expends energy on the problem it *thinks* is most important. If stressful events occur while you are eating — family arguments, loud noises, listening to upsetting news bulletins — energy and activity in the gut may slow down, or even turn off altogether.

If you are stressed, alcohol is the last thing you should resort to for relaxation or release. It is a stimulant, not a relaxant. If stress is causing you sleeping problems, it will create a double whammy effect. Like some sleeping pills, alcohol depresses the brain systems that control wakefulness. As its effects wear off, a wake rebound reaction occurs. This causes restlessness and fragmented sleep. It also increases the chances of waking up in the middle of a dream. Alcohol is metabolised at the rate of about one drink per hour. So if you are drinking in the evening, you'll need about four hours to metabolise four drinks.

Drinking alcohol is a bad idea if you are flying. Alcohol consumed while flying at 30,000 feet is two to three times stronger than the equivalent amount consumed on the ground. Alcohol also exacerbates the dehydration problem associated with air travel.

For those who are not stressed, the medical profession's general recommendation is that men should not exceed twenty-one units and women fourteen units per week of alcohol. One unit is the equivalent of a pint of beer, or one glass of wine. (For further information on the effects of alcohol, see *Sleep: The CommonSense Approach*.)

CHAPTER 10

Medication

A ccording to consultant psychiatrist, Dr Abbie Lane, medication has a very small part to play in stress management. It's really only for those who have developed depression. As few as fifteen per cent of people suffering from stress will develop psychiatric, or psychological, symptoms serious enough to require medication.

The most common manifestations of depression are sleeping problems, a feeling of hopelessness, suicidal thoughts, severe loss of appetite, with or without weight loss and poor concentration. If those symptoms have persisted for more than two weeks, then medical intervention is called for.

Anti-depressants, beta-blockers and benzodiazepines (tranquillisers and sleeping pills) are the main forms of medication used. You can expect anti-depressants (which have a sleep-inducing side effect) to work for months, but the maximum effectiveness period for sleeping pills tends to be *weeks* rather than months. While they have an important role to play in helping people with sleeping disorders, sleeping pills are not for the long haul.

Tranquillisers

Modern psychiatric practice recommends limiting the prescription of tranquillisers (one of the two major types of benzodiazepines) to patients with severe, very disabling or incapacitating stress reactions, because tranquillisers are addictive.

Beta-blockers, on the other hand, which significantly reduce anxiety levels and tension, can be useful in one-off situations, such as helping someone get through a major perform-ance, or anticipated traumatic event. They are non-addictive, quick acting and relatively inexpensive. One caution, however. Specific side effects include dizziness and low blood pressure, caused by their impact on cardiac function.

Anti-Depressants

For someone experiencing debilitating feelings of crisis, hope-lessness, sleep disturbance or suicidal thoughts, the most appropriate medication is either a tricyclic anti-depressant, or one of the newer SSRI group of anti-depressants.

Most anti-depressants take between two and four weeks to become effective. Most have an anxiolytic (anxiety reduc-ing/muscle relaxing) effect, and are non-addictive. They may be used long term, but are usually prescribed for a defined period of time, tailored to an individual's needs. Patients are usually weaned off them rather than stopped abruptly.

Most anti-depressants have some side effects, ranging from dry mouth, constipation and urinary problems (in men with prostate trouble), to nausea, intermittent blurred vision, day-time drowsiness, to restlessness and jumpiness. These are just rough guidelines, because individual reactions vary enormously — from no reaction in people on whacking doses, to debilitating reactions in people on tiny doses. You may also have to monitor your alcohol intake and be careful about driving or operating machinery. Check with your doctor for guidelines on this.

SSRIs have fewer side effects and are less sedative, but are more expensive than tricyclics. They are also stimulating, and can sometimes *increase* sleeping problems and thereby increase stress. For this reason, they are not suitable for patients suffering from a form of depression in which sleeping problems are also manifesting.

However, the most common scenario is one where a patient is suffering from a combination of depression and sleeping problems. Then they may be prescribed a combination of anti-depressants and sleeping pills.

A Word of Caution about Sleeping Pills

1 There is no such thing as an ideal sleeping pill. The same medication can create completely different reactions in different people.

2 Even though they may be described as, say, six-hour action (i.e. give you six hours sleep), that may actually manifest itself as three hours in one person and ten in another, depending on age and existing medical conditions.

3 As already emphasised, they are only ever a short-term solution — maybe for as little as three weeks, depending on the individual and the frequency with which they're taken (e.g. nightly, every second/third night). If taken nightly, they are more likely to become ineffective.

4 Because they can be psychologically and physically addictive, getting people off them is difficult, so generally it's best not to get started.

5 Some sleeping pills linger on in the system for up to twenty-four hours, and may affect psycho-motor functions such as operating machinery or driving. In addition, the effect on short-term memory can be terrible.

CHAPTER 11

Alternative Therapies

Aromatherapy

Aromatherapy is an excellent way of dealing with stress and its symptoms, although obviously only a change in life style and mental attitude can actually eliminate the cause.

Stress often brings an increased desire for smoking, eating (or not eating!), excessive drinking of coffee or alcohol, and perhaps taking medication. These are only temporary 'comforting' aids: all of them can, unfortunately, lead to over-use and become difficult habits to break.

According to Shirley Price, author of six books on Aromatherapy and regarded as one of the world's leading experts on this subject, regular use of certain essential oils can help lessen the desire for those so-called comforts, as they are a true comfort to anyone under stress. They can be used in many different ways; and even when stress is not a major factor in your life, they are a very practical method of maintaining health and vitality.

Shirley Price adds that, contrary to popular belief, massage isn't necessarily an integral part of aromatherapy; although massage itself can relieve stress, essential oils can be used effectively in several other ways to alleviate the physical and psychological effects of stress. For example:

◆ In stressful one-off situations such as just before a job interview, or shortly after receiving bad news, inhalation is most effective. (Simply put six to eight drops on a tissue and inhale deeply.)

◆ In situations where stress is on-going, a combination of inhalation and aromatic baths should work well. The recommendation there is to add six to eight drops of a combination of two or three different oils to a bath, making sure they are well dispersed in the water.

◆ Having a partner or a qualified aromatherapist give you a neck and shoulder massage would be ideal, but if that is not an option, then essential oils applied to your neck and shoulders also work quite well for on-going stress. To make up a small quantity, add four drops of essential oils diluted in two teaspoonfuls of non-greasy base lotion or vegetable oil.

Stress often impairs one's sleeping pattern, so, by reducing the stress, better sleep should follow automatically. In such cases, take a ten-minute bath with essential oils added, inhale oils from a tissue or vaporiser (burner) at least half an hour before going to bed, and follow this by self-application of the same mix of oils to the shoulders and neck before retiring.

Using a vaporiser generally is also worth considering. If one is not to hand, place twelve drops of essential oils with plenty of water in a saucer and leave it in the office, or the room at home where you spend most of your time. However, saucers are really only effective when put in a warm place, e.g. on a sunnywindowsill or radiator. An alternative is to put some oils on a tissue and insert it in a shirt pocket. As the heat of the body vaporises the oils, the vapour rises to your nostrils. Most efficient of all is a glass diffuser, although these can be difficult to find.

In times of stress, the neck and shoulder areas tend to be very tense. This is because stress over-stimulates the sympathetic nervous system, thereby forcing muscles to become tense. By using a combination of massage and essential oils, the para-sympathetic nervous system can be brought back to normal. The six steps in the self-massage process are as follows:

1 Stroke your left shoulder firmly, in circular movements, with the whole of your relaxed right hand. Your hand should be draped over your shoulder.
2 Push your fingers into the tight muscles on and behind the shoulder. The tight muscle areas will hurt, so these will be easy to find. Make small, firm circles over the painful areas.
3 Repeat the stroking movement over the whole shoulder.
4 Take your hand up the side of your neck, making circular movements again with your fingers, and finish behind the ear.
5 Repeat step 1 again.
6 Repeat the whole sequence with the left hand on the right shoulder.

In using essential oils, Shirley Price emphasises several points. Firstly, you need to understand that they are not oils in the conventional sense, although they do not easily dissolve in water. Rather, they are the distilled essences of flowers, leaves, bark, resins or gums. It takes huge quantities of these raw materials to manufacture the finished product. 150–200 kilos of lavender will give about one litre of essential oil: the same amount of orange blossoms will yield only about 20 ml (about a thimbleful) of neroli. All essential oils are extremely potent, so you should treat them with respect.

Aromatherapy is a highly individualised process. Whereas actual skin penetration may take only a matter of minutes, it can take anything from half an hour to twelve hours for the oils to reach the organs through the blood and the lymphatic system, depending on the individual.

If you are pregnant, certain oils may be contra-indicated, so seek the advice of a properly qualified aromatherapist first. People with epilepsy may also be precluded from using certain essential oils.

Always purchase quality oils only, and find out whether or not they have already been diluted with a carrier oil. If they have, they can be used for application directly on to the skin. However, they would not be suitable for use in a vaporiser or on a tissue. For bath use, you would require half the contents of a 10 ml bottle to create the equivalent effect of about six to eight drops of the pure essential oil. When mixing your own oils for application or massage, you will need sixteen drops in 50 ml of vegetable oil or white base lotion.

Because aromatherapy is so highly individualised, an oil that creates a relaxing effect in one person may actually have a stimulating effect on another. For that reason, it is best to combine two or three oils at one go.

After an aromatherapy massage, avoid taking a shower or bath for at least three or four hours after treatment, to ensure full absorption.

The following is Shirley Price's recommended list of oils to counteract stress symptoms. Use two or three from any one list to combat the particular symptom, and find common oils if suffering from more than one symptom. For example, for irritability, muscle tension and insomnia, the common oils are sweet marjoram and juniper. If muscle tension and/or insomnia are the leading symptoms, lavender could be added; or any other essential oil from the irritability section if that is the leading symptom.

- cypress, geranium, juniper, mandarin, sweet marjoram and bitter orange for *irritability*
- geranium, sweet marjoram, true melissa, neroli, patchouli, petitgrain and rosewood for *emotional instability*
- Roman chamomile, juniper, lavender and sweet marjoram for *muscle tension* in various parts of the body, but mainly in the neck or shoulders
- Roman chamomile, cypress, juniper, lavender, sweet marjoram, true melissa, rose otto, sandalwood and ylang ylang for *insomnia*

- Roman chamomile, eucalyptus smithii, lavender, sweet marjoram, peppermint and rosemary for *headaches* and *migraines*
- lemon, peppermint and rosemary for *inability to concentrate*
- black pepper, Roman chamomile, caraway, ginger, mandarin, peppermint and sandalwood for *nausea* and *indigestion*.

Herbal Medicine

According to Dublin-based medical herbalist Helen McCormack, certain herbs play a supportive role in helping to raise tolerance to stress, while others reduce physical and nervous tension. Despite their usefulness, however, she would rarely prescribe this medication in isolation. It would almost always be accompanied by advice on adopting more healthy life style habits, with specific directives on diet, exercise, yoga or other relaxation techniques.

The herbal big guns in the stress battle armoury include borage, chamomile, damiana, ginseng, hops, motherwort, oats, Siberian ginseng, skullcap, St John's wort, valerian, vervain and wood betony. All of them are considered excellent for the nervous system and have a variety of therapeutic actions. Certain ones (valerian, St John's wort and skullcap) have a calming effect and are useful in helping those suffering from anxiety and tension. They may combine well with passion flower, if stress has resulted in sleeping problems.

Oats are an excellent tonic and restorative for the nervous system; they are indicated for people suffering from nervous exhaustion.

Motherwort is excellent for nervous excitability and, as its name implies, is often indicated for women who may be experiencing anxiety/depression as a result of hormonal swings with menstrual or menopausal origins. It also helps relieve palpitations of nervous origin.

Vervain has an anti-spasmodic action and relieves muscle tension. It has overall beneficial effects on the liver and kidneys and acts as a general tonic.

Damiana acts as a stimulating tonic for the nervous system and can relieve depression and anxiety states. This herb has a particular reputation in relation to the treatment of anxiety states with a sexual component.

Both *ginseng* and *Siberian ginseng* have a reputation as *the* herbs for stressful conditions. They are considered to have an adaptogenic action. In other words, they help the body adapt to the demands placed on it by improving its capacity for mental and physical exertion. They aid concentration, boost the body's immune system and enhance recuperative powers.

Siberian ginseng has a similar action to the better-known *Panax ginseng*. It is perhaps even more stimulating, and has an excellent reputation for improving stamina and increasing vitality.

Some people regard various forms of ginseng almost as daily dietary supplements, but Helen McCormack recommends that consumption be limited to periods of two to four weeks at a time only, and coffee should be avoided altogether while on a course.

Borage is believed to support the adrenal glands and is often recommended for people who have been on steroid therapy. It helps relieve depression and raises the spirits.

Valerian has an excellent tranquillising action which in no way impairs mental or physical function. It is calming without being notably sedating. It is excellent for all anxiety states and conditions caused by nervous tension.

Skullcap and *wood betony* are prescribed for those suffering from tension headaches.

Prolonged stress can play havoc with your digestive system, and medical herbalists may choose from a range of herbal prescriptions. *Chamomile* is often chosen for its soothing, anti-spasmodic properties because it aids digestion and prevents irritation. *Peppermint* is excellent for colic pains.

Hops are useful for 'nervous' stomach complaints such as diarrhoea and anxiety-related intestinal cramps and insomnia. Hops also calm digestive over-activity. They are contra-indicated in cases of depression and for those with a history of depression.

Carminatives including aniseed, caraway, fennel, angelica and lemon balm, ease flatulence and discomfort.

The herbs *Echinacea angustifolia* and *E. purpurea* have always had a reputation for boosting the body's natural resistance to infections. When the body is under stress, extra strain is placed on the immune system and the incidence of infections tends to increase. Echinacea has a positive effect on the body's defences to viral and fungal infections, as well as bacterial infections.

While Echinacea is useful for many types of infections, both viral and bacterial, a lot of people tend to use it as a daily prophylactic. However this can have the effect of undermining its overall efficiency. Taking Echinacea should be limited to times when the body is fighting the early stages of an infection, or during particularly stressful periods. It may also be a good idea to take it for a couple of weeks coming into wintertime, in order to build up our natural immunity.

Echinacea apart, Helen McCormack sounds a general note of warning about the temptation to self-medicate without detailed knowledge:

Most of the herbal remedies listed here are widely available in health food stores and pharmacies. Many will sound familiar to anyone who knows a little bit about growing herbs for kitchen use. As a result of this familiarity, however, there is a danger they may be perceived as pretty harmless. Quite the opposite: a lot of them are *very* potent.

About thirty per cent of pharmaceutical preparations derive from plants, yet herbal remedies aren't always regarded with the same caution and respect afforded to those proprietary medicines. Treating one of the remedies I have listed here as if it were some sort of a daily dietary supplement like cod liver oil capsules is downright silly. I would say self-medication with herbal remedies is fine as long as you know what you're doing. However, they should be treated just like any other medication, and it is always a good idea to seek the advice of a properly qualified medical herbalist before embarking on a course of treatment.

See Useful Addresses, pages 110–12, for details of referral contact points.

Making a herbal infusion or tea is the easiest way to take herbal medicine, and as a general rule a generous teaspoon added to one cup of boiling water is the recommended dosage. Many medical herbalists may make up a more concentrated 'tincture' form of the herb, just for convenience. Most will prescribe a combination of herbs which have a complementary or synergistic action.

CHAPTER 12

Stress Management Techniques

ABC Relaxation Method

Clinical psychologist, Dr Tony Bates, recommends Dr Herbert Benson's ABC relaxation method to his patients. The principles are as follows.

Anatomy

Start by tensing the arm muscles in the body for two seconds. Then let the arms drop, and experience the loosening and warmth of that feeling for four seconds. Continue the same tensing/ relaxing sequence for the shoulders and the neck, following on down through the body, and repeating the same procedure separately for the chest, stomach, buttocks and lower limbs.

Having done this, you should experience *some*, but not complete, relaxation in your body.

Breathing

Now begin to focus your attention on your breathing. At this stage, the idea is not to change your breathing in any direction, either to speed it up or slow it down, but simply to observe its rhythm, and as you do, to notice that it will probably slow down slightly. As you observe the rhythm, pay particular attention to each time you exhale breath. Notice that as you exhale, and each time you exhale, your body relaxes a little more. Now you are loosening and feeling a warmth throughout your body. Your focus is on your breathing, and each time you breathe out, you allow your body to relax a little more.

Calm

While maintaining a relaxation within your body and a rhythm in your breathing, and allowing yourself to relax a little more each time you breathe out, focus your attention on your mind. Dr Benson recommends that you find a focus for your mind, which can otherwise be restless and easily distracted. He suggests the word 'one', 'calm', or a word that has some religious significance. Simply say this word privately to yourself each time you breathe out. In short, breathe out while allowing your body to relax, and say your chosen word within your mind.

Alexander Technique

The Alexander Technique has a particular relevance in the context of an effective stress management life style. While not promoted as a therapy, it is none the less regarded as therapeutic by its tens of thousands of practitioners worldwide. Its most vocal exponents tend to be people in the performing arts — actors, dancers and musicians. They practise it to improve body movement and performance.

Equally enthusiastic exponents of the Alexander Technique include business people, decision-makers, broadcasters, journalists, doctors, mothers and massage therapists. They say it helps their thinking become clearer and calmer; movement becomes freer and lighter, thus giving them more energy and stamina.

Included among those who benefit most are people with stress-related or stress-induced conditions, such as migraine sufferers; people suffering from repetitive strain or sports injuries; and most of all, those who suffer with back trouble. The technique is, in fact, endorsed by the Back Pain Associations of America and the UK.

In the psychological domain, chief beneficiaries include Type A personalities and people suffering from anxiety or social difficulties, including stammering and chronic shyness.

What is It and How Does It Work?

The Alexander Technique first became popular over one hundred years ago, and it has drifted in and out of fashion ever since. These days, there are 3,000 teachers worldwide. Before they are qualified to practise, they must spend at least 1,600 hours in intensive formal training. In terms of duration and intensity, training is on a par with many of the paramedical professions.

Describing the Alexander Technique, and how it is taught, are difficult. Its underlying philosophy is psycho-physical, but any notion that it is fringe or mystical should be dismissed. Fundamental to understanding the technique is an appreciation of the importance of the relationship of the head to the neck to the spine. The process involves the conscious re-direction of mental and physical activity. It is non-manipulative, however. Alexander Technique teachers simply teach you how to develop awareness and reduce effort in everyday activities (both physically and mentally), how to respond to situations in a non-habitual way, and how to direct your activity in a new and improved manner.

When practised properly, reactions to all the typical physiological stress responses are diminished, according to Mary Derbyshire, a US-based Alexander Technique teacher:

We guide you through very basic movements — sitting, standing, walking or lying down.

We demonstrate to you through our hands and verbal instruction how you are habitually interfering with your natural sense of poise and balance. By re-integrating the head, neck and spine, we re-educate your whole kinaesthetic sense. With this re-education comes a profound sense of lightness, freedom and choice.

The Alexander Technique is a cognitive process. At the core, the message is *think more, do less*. It can be described as preventing habitual responses of excessive muscular tension, and redirecting your activities in a profoundly new way. Between twenty and thirty one-to-one, twenty- to thirty-minute sessions, at roughly weekly intervals, are needed to learn the technique. No special clothes or equipment are required. Moreover, age, lack of physical fitness, or freedom of movement do not preclude a person from learning it. A willingness to change old habits is the only prerequisite.

Once learned, formal practice may be confined to two twenty-minute breaks every day, during which the person lies on the floor doing nothing at all. Informal practice is continuous, in the sense that use of the technique pervades every aspect of daily life. It is incorporated into the most mundane activities — driving a car, watching television, doing a job interview, sitting at an office desk or a computer.

In a stressful situation, its practice triggers the correct physiological responses. By keeping the head, neck and shoulders in the correct alignment, the body's reaction to the fight or flight response is diminished. Control, in all its most positive connotations, ensues more often than not.

Autogenic Training

Autogenic training is one of the most interesting mind-body control techniques around. One of the things that makes it so interesting is that it straddles two quite different roles — that of performance enhancer as well as chronic stress reducer.

For Type A personalities, it is particularly appropriate, as it is one of the most effective and comprehensive techniques for achieving profound relaxation. On the other hand, athletes, business people, pilots, writers, designers, musicians and doctors use it to improve performance and increase efficiency by sharpening their awareness and discernment. It helps some people become more decisive and solve problems positively. It can help others cope with seemingly impossible physical or mental feats. (Sportsmen pitted against extreme weather conditions, pain or exhaustion, fit into that latter category.)

Doctors, nurses, police officers, ambulance drivers, social workers and others in the caring professions use it to prevent the burn-out that can result from dealing constantly with emotionally exhausting situations. American and Russian astronauts have used it in their training to bring about physiological normalisation and aid relaxation.

What is Autogenic Training?

Autogenic means generated from within. The technique consists of a series of simple, easily learned mental exercises. These allow the body to calm itself by switching off its stress system. It has three components:

◆ passive concentration, quietly allowing the mind to focus on the body
◆ repetition of certain phrases to induce feelings of warmth and relaxation
◆ putting the body into positions designed to minimise distractions from the outside world.

Autogenics is not a quick fix — learning it requires patience and commitment. A course takes between eight and ten weeks, with one sixty- to ninety-minute class once a week. After that, all that's required is ten minutes' practice, three times a day. However, even one session a day can be helpful.

Autogenic Training is idiot-proof! Where it presents a challenge, it is in the discipline of practising three times a day. For most people, getting over the hurdle of doing something for themselves that frequently is a fantastic discipline, and in itself stops a build-up of frenetic activity throughout the day.

Autogenic Training is *not* meditation, with which it is frequently confused. The difference is that it induces specific normalising processes in the body–mind rather than trying to transcend them, as in the case of meditation. All the time you are doing Autogenic Training, you are totally aware.

Essentially, it is a form of self-regulation, used to bring about profound relaxation and relief from the negative effects of stress.

It can alter one's personality, but for the better. For example, it brings about release of creativity and greater emotional resilience. One of its other main benefits is reduced anxiety; this has been shown to be still active eight months after a course is over.

Who Can Benefit?

Autogenics is particularly helpful to people dealing with bereavement or other forms of loss. It enables them to functionally adjust to the deep psychological processing that follows a bereavement, marital separation or a major relationship break-up. It increases ego strength and brings cohesion to psychological fragmentation.

The scientific evidence weighted in favour of AT is impressive. There are some 3,000 studies demonstrating its effectiveness in the treatment of a wide range of disorders, including high blood pressure, asthma, irritable bowel syndrome and colitis, arthritis, muscular pain and tension, migraines, bladder disorders, sexual dysfunction, cardiac arrhythmias, angina, mild thyroid disorders, epilepsy, pain relief in childbirth, premenstrual tension, digestive disturbances and sleep problems.

Other areas where the autogenic process can help include reactive depression, panic attacks, unresolved grief reactions, anxiety disorders and phobias.

Dr Alice Greene, a Harley Street homeopathic doctor and Vice-Chairwoman of the British Association for Autogenic Training and Therapy (BAFATT), says that the people who benefit most are typically over-stretched, ambitious, stressed, competitive, impatient, restless, high achievers, or those with 'hurry sickness'. It brings about a profound shift in their personalities. Their adrenalised state disappears as a result of the physiological and psychological consequences that Autogenics brings about. By re-balancing the body's autonomic nervous system, the net effects it produces are reduced heart rate, lower blood pressure and breathing rate, less sweating, increased gut movement and improved digestion.

The kind of change achieved by autogenics corresponds in large part to those changes produced by medications designed to reduce anxiety. However, it doesn't feature any of their disadvantages, or quality of life inhibitors. Under proper super-vision, autogenics can help wean people off tranquillisers, sleeping pills and anti-depressant drugs. But it can also be used safely in parallel with those medications until either it or the effects of a counselling process begin to kick in.

Technically, it is possible to learn autogenics from a book but that is not recommended. Transient emotional off-loadings are part of the process, so it is essential to have access to a properly qualified trainer while this is going on. All members of BAFATT, for example, will have been through a three-year specialist training programme. A separate qualification in medicine, nursing, counselling, psychology or occupational therapy is also a prerequisite for acceptance on one of their training programmes.

Is it Appropriate for Everyone?

Not every patient is suitable for autogenic training. Dr Greene stresses that pre-course evaluation is a prerequisite for deter-mining a patient's selection. Those precluded are patients on major tranquillisers, those suffering with schizophrenia, psychoses or endogenous depression. Diabetics who are not under medical supervision are also precluded, because it can bring about a reduction in their need for insulin. Others precluded are those whose medical history is not available, or who refuse to give it, people with severe chest pain (where there may be an impending heart attack) and children under the age of five.

Although people with severe endogenous depression are precluded, those with reactive depression may find it very useful. Post-heart-attack patients also find it a very helpful rehabilitation therapy. Autogenics is actually cardio-protective, because it reduces stress, lowers lipids, increases coronary blood blow and reduces blood pressure and heart rate.

Once learned, autogenics is never forgotten. It can be practised anywhere in any circumstances — while stuck in traffic, killing time in an airport, or hurtling through the air in an aircraft at 500 miles an hour. A quiet atmosphere, subdued lighting and warmth are probably best for beginners, however.

See Useful Addresses, pages 110–12, for referral contact points.

Breathing

Out of the eleven systems in the body, the only one we can control voluntarily is breathing. Most people don't know how to breathe properly, however. The kind of shallow breathing we use every day is worlds apart from the diaphragmatic breathing essential for deep relaxation and stress management.

In cases where stress is managed poorly or not at all, muscles are continuously tightened in preparation for the fight-or-flight stress response and, over time, they shrink. In tandem with that, the diaphragm also gradually tightens and shrinks. In very severe cases, where people are subjected to intimidation and fear for prolonged periods, fundamental physiological changes take place. Body shape can alter, as muscle shrinkage literally causes the chest area to develop a concave shape. Thereafter, a rigid, hunched body position is maintained.

Learning deep, diaphragmatic breathing is the first step in any successful stress management process. It is possible to learn it from a book, but having a professional show you how to do it works best. Clair Bel-Maguire is a physical well-being therapist who specialises in stress management training courses. The breathing technique that she teaches is designed to bring down heart rate, lower blood pressure and reduce generalised anxiety. It helps lessen irritability, alleviates headaches and fights fatigue.

The Technique

Clair Bel-Maguire's technique differs from those described in most books, in that she recommends trying to do it with as little effort as possible. 'It is a simple process and should be regarded as such,' she says. It can be practised either lying down or sitting in a chair.

Taking the lying down option first:

1 Place one hand on your tummy, the other on your chest.
2 Breathe in through your nose for a count of five; then out for a count of five.
3 As you breathe in for a count of five, the tummy should rise, and as you breathe out for a count of five, it should deflate.

If lying on the floor is not an option, use a chair with an armrest:

1 Sit well back in the seat, two feet firmly planted on the floor, but well apart; arms on the rest and eyes closed.
2 Begin by breathing through your nose and out through your mouth very slowly; tongue resting on the bottom of mouth, teeth and lips apart, shoulders dropped.

For the best results, this breathing routine needs to be practised for least five minutes three times a day, first thing in the morning, last thing at night and at another time of your choice.

Jacobson's Relaxation Technique

This technique is simple to learn, and its effects are gradual. It works by retraining the relaxation reflexes, and involves the systematic tightening and loosening of all the muscle groups in the body, one after the other. As a result, deep muscle relaxation occurs. This spreads to other body systems, thereby producing a profound reduction in physiological tension and psychological anxiety.

There is no mystery about this technique. It is neither new nor revolutionary. It is widely used in maternity hospitals for birthing classes, and is one of the most commonly recorded techniques found on commercial audio relaxation tapes. It can also be learned from a book.

The technique is to isolate and tighten a muscle group as hard as you can without pain; hold it for five to seven seconds and then relax. A typical sequence would be: feet, calf muscles, thighs, buttocks/pelvic area, stomach, back, hands, arms, shoulders, neck, face/head, eyes, teeth/jaws. All the time you are doing this, you practise deep breathing.

This tensing and relaxing sequence is then followed by a short period of lying quietly.

It requires one or two ten- to fifteen-minute sessions of uninterrupted time in a quiet place, over a one- or two-week period, before the benefits become apparent.

Massage

Apart from relaxing muscles, relieving tension and making you feel good, massage creates a huge number of positive physiological effects. These include acting as a 'mechanical cleanser', stimulating lymph circulation, hastening the elimination of wastes and toxic debris, removing the adrenaline residue that can otherwise lay down plaque in the arteries, dilating blood vessels, improving circulation, relieving congestion throughout the body, and aiding digestion.

It can also be enormously helpful in the treatment of repetitive strain injury or over-use syndrome, a very common complaint with people who spend long periods sitting in front of computers or who have poor posture. It can help with tension headaches, insomnia, back or neck pain. It is also beneficial for people who through injury or illness are unable to exercise regularly. Massage helps relax contracted muscles and tone others that may be over-stretched and weak.

Less well recognised are its diagnostic benefits. In an ideal world, almost everyone would incorporate massage into their self-care routine, just like dental or medical check-ups — except more frequently.

All muscles shorten and contract when they are stressed. And because all stress manifests in muscle, and will display certain patterns as a result, a skilled physical therapist is able to identify what the source is. Massage can help pinpoint quickly where problem areas exist. Regular visits (once a month) would be considered ideal, as stress may manifest unbeknownst to you within a few short weeks.

Irrespective or origin, no muscle area can be viewed in isolation. All muscles work in pairs. So, stressed and contracted muscles in one area have a knock-on effect elsewhere. For example, one of the most common symptoms of workplace stress is tension in the head, neck and shoulders area. If not dealt with, something as apparently innocuous as a frequently clenched jaw can cause referred pain and lead to severe headache, ear ache or neck pain. This often leads to a lot of tests and investigations, some of which can be invasive.

So, now you know why the wrong kind of meetings or encounters with really difficult people can literally give you a pain in the neck!

Apart from the knock-on effect created by stressed muscles passing on tension to other parts of the body, contracted muscles retain toxins. Obviously, retaining toxins in the body is undesirable anyway, but more than this, they actually impede muscle performance and may create a whole set of other problems.

Meditation

Sometimes doing nothing is doing something very important.

Dr Michael DelMonte is a senior clinical psychologist and psychotherapist, and one of the world's leading authorities on meditation. He describes it as a special state, facilitated by physical relaxation — a temporary haven, rather than an escape from life.

On the face of it, it looks like you are doing nothing while meditating, but this is deceptive. The physical stillness required for the meditative process can facilitate mental stillness. One of the most consistent benefits of meditation is reduced anxiety, and there are dozens of good research studies to show this. Its practice can also help self-actualisation — the sense of how fulfilled we feel.

For someone with a very busy and stressful life, meditation is an antidote to the constant buzz and bombardment of stimulation. It is not suitable, however, for people who are already very withdrawn, or who have serious mood swings, depressions or psychoses, or have problems with addictive or impulsive behaviour (e.g. bulimia).

According to Dr DelMonte meditation allows you to get out of the fast lane for a bit. The recommended practice is two daily twenty-minute sessions, sitting upright in a chair in quiet, comfortable surroundings, with closed eyes, while silently repeating a mantra, or any soothing sound which can be used to dislodge our endless internal chatter.

The main benefits of meditation are that it teaches people skills like concentration, absorption, self-observation and singleness of thought. It helps them become less distracted, more focused, receptive, and non-judgmental. It also has a role in helping people with mild hypertension and insomnia. It can assist others give up soft drug habits like smoking, drinking or using other recreational drugs.

Dr DelMonte explains that there are two main techniques: concentration and mindfulness.

Concentrative meditation is basically a training in very narrowly focused attention. On the other hand, mindfulness meditation is the practice of panoramic or wide-angle attention, where your mind is open to everything, with an attitude of 'choiceless awareness'. However, you cannot practise mindfulness properly until you have mastered concentration.

The first step is to learn concentration (attentional skills). Practically all the schools of meditation, whatever their origin, teach some type of prolonged concentration. Any of the five senses can be used to focus on aspects of the environment or on yourself (e.g. on your breathing or walking). However, you can also meditate on mental imagery. In one of the most common forms of meditation, focused concentration is achieved by sub-vocally repeating a mantra in a monotonous manner.

A mantra is like an island in a sea of thought. Sometimes the mantra has a meaning, but often the sound is meaningless, neutral but pleasant. By focusing on the mantra sound, the practitioner creates a mental discipline, stillness and focus. If you repeat the sound over and over again, the mind switches off because it is programmed to look for 'news of a difference'. Concentrative meditation naturally brings monotony. After a while, you cannot hear the mantra. This is called 'no thought' — it is a special type of adaptive dissociation, or trance.

People strive for 'no thought', because when the mind turns off and nothing happens, this creates a psychological space. That empty space is like a fertile silence, in which something new can emerge. In creating such a space, you are then open to receiving something beyond or below thought. That 'beyond thought' experience, 'being at one', may eventually convert into serenity, tranquillity or 'nirvana'. It is difficult to achieve this serenity, but ultimately, this is what most medi-tation is about.

The road to eventual serenity may be interrupted, while previously blocked emotions are released. These emotions were often subconsciously repressed, i.e. 'below thought'. Many people become good at meditation in time. They can even practise mini-meditations, by closing their eyes in an office and quietening down their minds momentarily. Often, if they are quite agitated, they may emerge after ten to fifteen minutes of practice looking and feeling quite tranquil.

Yoga

A few years ago, the sight of large numbers of high-powered British lawyers and computer company executives downing tools and slipping into track suits to practise yoga during their forty-five-minute lunch break would have been considered preposterous.

Such is the acceptance and esteem in which it is held by millions of practitioners worldwide, however, that corporate yoga classes for executives and shift workers are no longer pass remarkable. Shift workers are, in fact, an interesting case in point. Many experience a variety of circadian rhythm disorders, and one by-product of yoga is that twenty minutes' practice may equate to four hours' sleep, while at the same time helping the body re-adjust to other rhythms, such as eating.

Yoga is recognised as one of the most perfect antidotes to the worst excesses of modern life. For many healthcare pro-fessionals, people suffering from information overload and those leading a life style of relative physical inactivity combined with bad posture and periods of stress, it is a lifeline.

It may also be their only route to self-awareness, a funda-mental for effective self-care, because one of the first things you learn if you join a yoga class is where stress is retained in the body. That 'where' is different for everybody, and knowing its location enables you to devise specific counteracting measures.

Yoga and Stress

Yoga is an ideal way to achieve deep relaxation and fitness, without ever getting out of breath. It uses slow, gentle movements and stretches to exercise every part of the body, release energy and remove tension. It focuses particularly on the spine, which houses the central nervous system. This is one of the reasons why it is especially good for helping a range of nervous conditions, such as stress, anxiety and tension.

The second major component of yoga is breathing. In times of stress, the diaphragm becomes rigid, and breathing becomes shallow. About half the time spent in a typical yoga class is focused on breathing techniques to relax the diaphragm and calm and soothe the mind. Once learned, those same techniques can be applied later if preparing for confrontation, or if you find yourself caught up in a stressful situation unexpectedly.

For busy people, one of its main advantages is that it is not as time consuming as other exercise regimes. A single one-and-a-half-hour class once a week is sufficient to keep you in gear, but this may, of course, lead to more regular practice.

Joints and muscles that are not used often enough just don't work anymore. They become stiff, and age. Amongst other things, back pain and shoulder pain may ensue. Yoga teaches the correct posture, to stave off the kind of problems that may arise if muscles are not managed properly. The other plus is that because stress tends to mask your personality with anger and negativity, it may prevent your full, positive self from emerging. Yoga peels away those layers of tension, and so the core 'you' should emerge.

Linda Southgate has been teaching yoga for sixteen years, and argues that no one should be prevented from practising by extreme youth, old age, lack of fitness or disability.

Of the total 80,000 movements, I only use twenty or thirty in a normal class. Certain postures are precluded for people with high blood pressure or ulcers, and I modify some for women at certain stages of pregnancy or people with back pain, but that's about it as far as contra-indications go. People take responsibility for their own bodies, and therefore empower themselves to know what is right for their own particular needs.

Most people will opt to do a ten-week course, with each class lasting one and a half hours. There is no obligation to re-enrol after a course, but most people continue by choice. They are motivated purely by the benefits they derive for everyday living. After a while, better posture, and therefore a less stressed body, become automatic. Likewise, you learn to automatically associate certain breathing techniques with a telephone ringing or seeing a red traffic light.

Outside the weekly class period, people can choose to practise certain *asanas* (movements) at home, in the office, or while driving. Yoga can be strenuous, but everyone exercises at their own pace. One of its lesser known features is that it can help achieve weight loss and change of body shape while maintaining a good level of fitness. Overall, the most common report is, 'I'm coping much better now,' but then stress is an internal response anyway, isn't it?

CHAPTER 13

Centres of Expertise

B y now, the message that chronic stress can lead to chronic
ill health may seem laboured. But while stress is a serious
issue, it is also a slippery subject, with many manifestations and
interpretations. Centres with particular expertise in stress
management are few and far between. Two such locations are
the Dublin County Stress Clinic and the Centre for Stress
Management in London (see Useful Addresses, pages 110–12).
Both use a multi-disciplinary approach, and employ teams of
highly trained counsellors, psychologists and psychotherapists.
Among the myriad techniques taught in both clinics are:

◆ assertiveness and communication skills
◆ building self-esteem
◆ time management
◆ ways to recognise sources of stress in your life and to
  understand your own stress reactions
◆ ways to manage pressure and stress, including relaxation
  techniques, problem solving and getting a good perspective
  on issues.

The Dublin County Stress Clinic

This clinic differs from many other stress management centres,
in that it offers the services of a consultant psychiatrist and
a team of other specialists, including clinical psychologists,
family therapists, cognitive behaviour therapists, a physical
well-being therapist and a clinical sports psychologist.

A comprehensive clinical assessment is provided for every client, and then an individually tailor-made programme is provided. The types of problems treated include anxiety, panic attacks, depression, occupational stress, relationship issues, post-traumatic stress disorder, acute stress reaction and phobias. Most clients are individually treated, but group programmes are also run.

The Dublin centre runs an eight-week, group-based stress management course, with each three-hour class divided equally between instruction in psychological techniques and progressive relaxation and exercise sessions. For enrolment, a letter from a GP is a prerequisite, partly to ensure that other physiological causes or stress symptoms mimicry have already been investigated.

The Centre for Stress Management

The Centre for Stress Management doesn't work with groups or run courses at its London headquarters, although it does provide tailor-made courses and stress audits for organisations on location. Its main focus is on individual stress counselling and stress management coaching for those suffering from stress, anxiety and a range of other difficulties such as high blood pressure.

This centre offers clients a range of services, including cognitive therapy, rational emotive behaviour therapy, problem focused therapy and multi-modal therapy (a form of cognitive behaviour therapy, which takes a holistic approach). For those unable to travel, a distance learning (correspondence) course on how to manage stress is available.

Health professionals, including doctors, psychotherapists, psychiatrists and psychologists travel from all over the world to do stress management and stress counselling training courses at the London centre. It also has a large mail order section, selling books and videos on health-related matters.

CHAPTER 14

Choosing a Therapist

*When writing isn't enough, you need to talk to somebody
and when talking isn't enough, you need a psychotherapist.*

P sychotherapy is often confused with psychiatry. However,
you don't have to be mentally ill to seek counselling.
Counselling is more short term, directive, crisis oriented and
supportive. Psychotherapy is something which attempts to
explore the underlying differences that give rise to behaviour or
mood problems. Psychotherapists do not administer psycho-
active drugs. Essentially, they help people to make sense of their
internal emotional lives, and their relationships.

There are many different branches of psychotherapy.
Among the principal branches are the following, according to
the UK Council for Psychotherapy:

◆ cognitive and behavioural therapy
◆ constructivist psychotherapy
◆ family therapy
◆ humanistic and integrative psychotherapy
◆ psychoanalytic psychotherapy.

Choosing the right therapist can be a whole new stressor in its
own right, but sorting out a few fundamental issues can help
ease this tricky process somewhat.

Whichever branch of psychotherapy you choose, it is essential to pick someone who is experienced, well trained and, most
importantly, a 'decent human being'. Other key characteristics

include the ability to listen intelligently and refrain from making simplistic or dogmatic statements. The therapist should be someone you feel safe with; who gives constructive feedback, without making you feel punished; someone you trust; who makes you feel understood and cared about; someone who makes sense of a problem in such a way that allows you to see it in a new light and act on it, rather than feel overwhelmed and helpless.

A good therapist will offer an interpretation of what is causing your problems at a pace and in a way you will understand. They should also be able to give you some sense of how long you will be in therapy, and the kind of process it will involve. They will offer hope.

Some may want you to write things down between sessions. Others may just want you to talk, while they remain silent. Still others may be highly interactive. There are many variations.

As a first step, you should establish what their particular style is, and then pick the one you're most comfortable with. A personal recommendation from a GP, clergyman, health authority professional or close friend is probably the easiest way to get the selection process moving.

The following checklist was developed by Dr Stephen Palmer and Kasia Szymanska, at the Centre for Stress Management, London.

1 Check that your counsellor has relevant qualifications and experience in the field of counselling/psychotherapy.
2 Ask about the type of approach the counsellor uses, and how it relates to your problem.
3 Ask if your counsellor is in supervision. (Most professional bodies consider supervision to be mandatory.)*
4 Ask if the counsellor, or counselling agency, is a member of a professional body and abides by a code of ethics. If possible, obtain a copy of the code.

5 Discuss your goals and expectations.

6 Ask about the fees, if any. If your income is low, check if the counsellor operates on a sliding scale. Discuss the frequency and estimated duration of the course.

7 Arrange regular review sessions with your counsellor to evaluate your progress.

8 Do not enter into a long-term counselling contract unless you are satisfied that this is necessary and beneficial to you.

* Counselling supervision is a formal arrangement where counsellors discuss their counselling in a confidential setting on a regular basis with one or more professional counsellors.

If you do not have a chance to discuss the above points during your first session, do so at the next possible opportunity.

General Pointers

Counsellor self-disclosure can sometimes be therapeutically useful. However, if the sessions are dominated by the counsellor discussing his or her own problems at length, raise this issue in the counselling session. If at any time you feel discounted, undermined or manipulated within the session, discuss this with the counsellor too. It is easier to resolve issues as and when they arise.

You should not accept significant gifts from your counsellor. This does not apply to relevant therapeutic material. Neither should you accept social invitations from your counsellor, for example, dining in a restaurant or going for a drink. However, this does not apply to relevant therapeutic assignments, such as being accompanied by your counsellor into a situation to help you overcome a phobia.

If your counsellor proposes a change in venue for the counselling sessions without good reason, do not agree: for example, from a centre to the counsellor's own home.

Research has shown that it is not beneficial for clients to have sexual contact with their counsellor. Professional counselling and psychotherapy bodies consider it unethical for counsellors, or therapists, to engage in a sexual relationship with current clients.

If you have any doubts about the counselling you are receiving, then discuss them with your counsellor. If you are still uncertain, seek advice — perhaps from a friend, your doctor, your local Citizens Advice Bureau, the professional body your counsellor belongs to, or the counselling agency that may employ your counsellor. If still unsure that you and the therapist are the right fit, a sensible guideline is to commit to no more than two or three sessions to establish whether this is a person with whom you are comfortable. Remember that you have the right to terminate counselling whenever you choose.

Cognitive Therapy

It is not possible within the constraints of a short book to describe all the various psychotherapies and how they work. Primarily for space and accessibility reasons, the rest of this chapter focuses on cognitive therapy.

This form of therapy is probably the most widely available. For example, more health authority clinical psychologists are trained in this discipline than any other. It is one of the most scientifically researched areas of psychotherapy. It is also short term — a typical course comprises twelve sessions over a twenty-week period, whereas psychoanalysis may take two years or longer.

Critics of cognitive therapy say that it is too short term and too problem-solving oriented. However, this apparent weakness is also one of its greatest strengths. For economic reasons, therapies have increasingly tended to be more short term, in any case. Cognitive therapy developed largely as a reaction to psychoanalysis, regarded by many as too long a process. One of the other criticisms levelled against the latter is that it isn't backed up by scientific research. It is particularly unstructured for people who are very depressed, which may not be helpful to them. However, for people with unresolved, unconscious issues that are not easily accessed, it may indeed be the best route.

What is Cognitive Therapy and Who Can It Benefit?

Cognitive therapy developed out of the simple notion that a major part of why we get upset is not just that life is awful, or very stressful. Rather, it's the *way* we interpret things and *how* we react to them that counts. Cognitive therapy tries to get at the geology of what is happening, not just what is appearing on the surface.

Cognitive therapy may be indicated when there is something happening to your emotional reactions that you can't quite pinpoint; where it happens recurrently and not exclusively in one particular environment, such as work. Sometimes the reasons may be apparent, but you can't talk about them easily. Or they may not be obvious to you, and they may make you feel you're going crazy because you don't understand why they're happening.

Behavioural signs such as overeating, drinking too much, drawing away from people, procrastinating, feeling constantly edgy, making poor decisions, feeling irritable, or getting stressed around specific things like sexuality — all are indications that you may need help.

Dr Tony Bates is a clinical psychologist, university lecturer and specialist in cognitive therapy. He says that he tries to help people become aware of the kinds of rules and attitudes towards living and behaving which they're often not aware they have.

Cognitive therapy is about helping people explore the *personal meaning* that key life events hold for them, and why they react to particular situations with unwarranted distress. Equipped with this self-awareness, and directed by specific self-help strategies, people can practise new ways of responding which are more effective. It helps them to find another way to see their problems, and discover creative solutions to these problems. It's also about helping them negotiate the world, adapt better, be more accepting of themselves and feel more contented.

Understanding Our Stress

This form of therapy is not about telling people to think positively — it is about *understanding* how we create much of our stress, and what we can do to reduce it and live more creatively. Cognitive therapy is also about beginning to put losses and stresses into words, so that the experiences can be digested and assimilated, Dr Bates adds.

At first, it may be very difficult to talk or write about historic hurts, but a number of studies show that it brings many benefits. For example, people who commit to keeping a diary and writing down upsetting events will show psychological, physiological and immunological improvements quicker. If done thoroughly and regularly (ten minutes a day for three weeks), this negative recording process will help put meaning on what is going wrong.

In other words, emotional processing of the events, feelings, thoughts and behaviours characterising life's bad moments *works*. Going through the same process and recording happy events, feelings and experiences does not, apparently, show any benefit in cases where reactions to stress have got out of hand.

Useful Addresses

Ireland

Autogenic Training
The Priory Clinic, 18 Priory Hall, Stillorgan, Co. Dublin.
Tel. 01 283 5566.

Aware — Helping to Defeat Depression
147 Phibsboro Road, Dublin 7. Tel. 01 830 8449.

Dublin County Stress Clinic
St John of God Hospital, Stillorgan, Co. Dublin.
Tel. 01 288 1781.

Institute of Physical Therapy
The Priory Clinic, 18 Priory Hall, Stillorgan, Co. Dublin.
Tel. 01 283 5566.

Irish Association for Counselling and Therapy
8 Cumberland Street, Dun Laoghaire, Co. Dublin.
Tel. 01 230 0061.

Irish Association of Medical Herbalists
186 Philipsburgh Avenue, Marino, Dublin 3. Tel. 01 836 7859.

Irish Council for Psychotherapy
17 Dame Court, Dublin 2. Tel. 01 679 4055.

Irish Yoga Association
108 Lower Kimmage Road, Harold's Cross, Dublin 6.
Tel. 01 492 9213.

Samaritans
112 Marlborough Street, Dublin 1. Tel. 01 872 7700; *or*
1850 60 90 90.

United Kingdom

AOC (Aromatherapy Organisations Council)
3 Latymer Close, Braybrooke, Market Harborough, Leicester
LE16 8LN. Tel. 01835 434242.

Association for Rational Emotive Behaviour Therapists
1 Jenkinson Close, Newcastle under Lyme, Staffordshire
ST5 2JP. Tel. 01782 631361.

British Association for Autogenic Training and Therapy
c/o The Royal London Homeopathic Hospital, Great Ormond
Street, London WC1N 3HR.
Postal enquiries only. Please send a stamped addressed
envelope for an information leaflet and a list of registered,
qualified practitioners.

British Association for Counselling
1 Regent Place, Rugby, Warwickshire CV21 2PJ.
Tel. 01788 578328.

British Psychological Society
St Andrew's House, 48 Princess Road East, Leicester
LE1 7DR. Tel. 0116 254 9568.

British Wheel of Yoga
BWY Central Office, 1 Hamilton Place, Boston Road,
Sleaford, Lincolnshire NG34 7ES. Tel. 01529 306851.

Centre for Stress Management
156 Westcombe Hill, Blackheath, London SE3 7DH.
Tel. 0181 293 4114.

Health Education Institute
Department of Oral Health and Development, University
Dental Hospital, Higher Cambridge Street, Manchester
M15 6FH.

Health Practitioners Association
Bretforton Hall Clinic, Bretforton, Vale of Evesham WR11 5JH.

Institute for Complementary Medicine
P. O. Box 194, London FE16 1QZ. Tel. 0171 237 5165.

International Society of Professional Aromatherapists (ISPA)
82 Ashby Road, Hinckley, Leicestershire LE10 1SN.
Tel. 01455 637 9987.

International Stress Management Association (UK)
Division of Psychology, South Bank University, 103 Borough
Road, London SE1 0AA. Tel. 07000 780430.

Manic Depression Fellowship
8 High Street, Kingston upon Thames, Surrey KT1 1EY.
Tel. 0181 974 6550.

MIND Information Line
Granta House, 15 Broadway, London E15.
Tel. 0181 522 1728; 0345 660163.

National Institute of Medical Herbalists
56 Longbrook Street, Exeter EX4 6AH. Tel. 01392 426022.

Northern Institute of Massage
100 Waterloo Road, Blackpool FY4 1AW. Tel. 01253 403548.

SANELINE
199 Old Marylebone Road, London NW1 5QP.
Tel. 0171 724 8000; 0345 678000.

Samaritans
10 The Grove, Slough, Berkshire. Tel. 01753 532713; *or*
0345 90 90 90.

Society of Teachers of the Alexander Technique
20 London House, 266 Fulham Road, London SW10 9EL.
Tel. 0171 351 0828.

United Kingdom Council for Psychotherapy
167 Great Portland Street, London W1. Tel. 0171 436 3002.

Further Reading

Benson, Herbert and Miriam Z. Klipper, *Relaxation Response*, New York: Avon Books 1976.

Berridge, J., C. L. Cooper and C. Highley, *Employee Assistance Programmes and Workplace Counselling*, New York: John Wiley & Sons Inc. 1997.

Borysenko, Joan, *Minding the Body, Mending the Mind*, New Jersey: Bantam Press 1993.

Boyne, Edward (ed.), *A Guide to Psychotherapy in Ireland*, Dublin: Columba Press 1993.

Burns, David D., *Feeling Good Handbook: Using the New Mood Therapy in Everyday Life*, Victoria: Plume Books 1989.

Cooper, Cary L. and Sue Cartwright, *Managing Workplace Stress*, London: Sage Publications 1997.

Cooper, Cary L., Rachel D. Cooper and Lynn H. Eaker, *Living with Stress*, London: Penguin 1987.

Covey, Stephen R., *Seven Habits of Highly Effective People: Powerful Lessons in Personal Change*, New Jersey: Simon & Schuster 1992.

Hayden, Fionnuala, *Whose Housework Is It Anyway?*, Dublin: Marino Press 1995.

Hopson, Barrie and Mike Scally, *Time Management: Conquer the Clock*, Mercury Business Books 1996.

Keane, Colm (ed.), *The Stress File*, Dublin: Blackwater Press 1997.

Keane, Colm, *Nervous Breakdown*, Dublin: Mercier Press 1994.

Kenton, Leslie, *10 Day De-stress Plan: Make Stress Work for You*, London: Ebury Press 1994.

Kenton, Susannah and Leslie Kenton, *Endless Energy: A Workbook for Dynamic Health and Personal Power for Women on the Move*, London: Vermilion 1993.

Kermani, Kai, *Autogenic Training: Effective Holistic Way to Better Health*, London: Souvenir Press 1996.

O'Hanlon, Brenda, *Sleep: The CommonSense Approach*, Dublin: Gill & Macmillan 1998.

Palmer, Stephen and Lynda Strickland, *Stress Management: A Quick Guide*, Cambridge: Daniels Medica 1995.

Palmer, Stephen and Tim Burton, *Dealing with People Problems at Work*, McGraw Hill.

Palmer, Stephen and Deborah Clarke, *How to Manage Stress*, National Extension College.

Peale, Norman Vincent, *Power of Positive Thinking*, Mandarin 1990.

Weekes, Claire, *Self Help for Your Nerves*, London: Thorsons 1995.

Weil, Andrew, *8 Weeks to Optimum Health*, London: Warner 1997.

Index

Stress